Developing a

Supernatural

Lifestyle

❦

A Practical Guide to a Life of Signs,
Wonders, and Miracles

Kris Vallotton

DESTINY IMAGE® PUBLISHERS, INC.
P.O. Box 310, Shippensburg, PA 17257-0310

*"Speaking to the Purposes of God for this
Generation and for the Generations to Come."*

This book and all other Destiny Image, Revival Press, Mercy Place,
Fresh Bread, Destiny Image Fiction, and Treasure House books
are available at Christian bookstores and distributors worldwide.

For a U.S. bookstore nearest you, call 1-800-722-6774.
For more information on foreign distributors, call 717-532-3040.
Or reach us on the Internet: **www.destinyimage.com**

ISBN 10: 0-7684-2501-8
ISBN 13: 978-0-7684-2501-7

For Worldwide Distribution, Printed in the U.S.A.
1 2 3 4 5 6 7 8 9 10 11/09 08 07

Dedication

———————————— ❧ ————————————

I dedicate this book to my seven grandchildren: Mesha, Elijah, Micah, Isaac, Rilie, Ella, and Evan. You are a voice to a generation that I will never see. You are my legacy, my greatest treasure, and the hope of a lost world stumbling in darkness in pursuit of their Creator. May we leave you a world in revival as your inheritance and may you always remember that I wrote every page of this book with you in mind.

I love you!

—Papa

Acknowledgments

◦

To my wife, Kathy—you are everything I thought you would be and more. Thank you for more than 31 years of pure joy.

To my children—Jaime and Marty, I am so proud of you. You have become great leaders. Shannon and Cameron, your lives inspire me and your marriage amazes me. Jason and Heather, your servanthood and humility set a high-water mark in the Body of Christ. Thank you for the way you always love me.

Gene, your life is a sign and a wonder—a testimony to the Father's loving grace.

Bill and Beni—You have taught us how to live. I am forever grateful.

Allison and Carol—Thank you for your hard work on this manuscript. You are both so gifted.

Nancy—Thanks for believing in me and praying for me.

Danny, Dann, Paul, Steve, Charlie, and Banning—You are my safety net and a lighthouse in the storms of my life.

Art and Cathy Kiperman—You were my first spiritual parents and I love you with all of my heart. Art, you have gone on to be with the Lord, but your life still lives on through me. May my heavenly treasure be assigned to your account.

Bill and Judy Derryberry—You guys are a bridge over troubled water and a safe harbor from the storms of life. Thousands owe their eternity to you.

Mom and Dad—Thank you both for loving me.

Bethel Church—You are the most amazing people on the face of the earth, truly a light set on a hill.

Endorsements

⌁

Thank you Kris, for another valuable book. One sign of a great teacher is that they walk the path of revelation yet know how to make the message easy to understand and apply so that others can walk there also. That is the gift that makes Bethel so valuable as a school and it comes largely from you Kris and Bill Johnson knowing how to take us with you on your journey. Please keep walking and talking and writing!

Dr. Lance Wallnau
Pastor and author

Kris Vallotton in his book, *Developing a Supernatural Lifestyle* has touched on many issues that need to be considered if one truly wants to live a consistent life of signs and wonders. Many people want the power, few what to live the life that justifies the Lord giving it to you. One must live the Word, not just talk about it.

John Paul Jackson
Founder, Streams Ministries International

We LOVE this book! *Developing A Supernatural Lifestyle* causes you to look at life from a new angle, and see God—the One who can do anything, anywhere through...you. Read it to become more of who you are created to be.

Wesley ande determination to pursue God's supernatural power. Both of these values bleed through the pages of this manuscript. Be careful as you read, you might be challenged to flee the comfort zone of religious mediocrity and pursue the destiny awaiting those tenacious enough to believe they can be history makers.

Larry Randolph
Larry Randolph Ministries

Kris Vallotton is not only an accurate prophet and a friend of God, but also a key pastor over the prophetic movement today. Kris is a covenant partner. We have experienced the fruit of his prophetic insight even in our own family. The Father desires us to live naturally supernatural lives as we lay our lives down for the King. May this book draw you into His heart, until you are so undone that you experience Heaven on earth.

Dr. Heidi G. Baker
Founding Director, Iris Ministries

Kris Vallotton is an amazing person, as is this book. The life of the Spirit pulsates through every page and challenges Christians to join Jesus in His mission to change the face of the whole world. For those looking for an easy escapism from the challenges of taking ground for Christ in the end times, this book offers you no place to hide.

Dr. Clay Ford
National Director of Holy Spirit Renewal Ministries

I first heard Kris speak at a conference in Toronto. I was gripped by his supernatural insight and wistful communication about the Kingdom of God. Like an eager travel agent, he takes multitudes across the chasm of unbelief into the relatively un-known realm of Heaven on earth. His humor and story telling abilities are his tools that build the bridges. *Developing a Super-natural Lifestyle* is a trail guide for the life we were created to live, but seldom experience.

Steve Witt
Pastor, Metro Church South, Cleveland, Ohio
Apostolic Team Member, Partners in Harvest, Toronto

Developing a Supernatural Lifestyle is the real deal. Kris leads "The School of the Supernatural" in Redding, California, a min-istry school that has produced radical disciples who are regularly healing the sick, casting out demons, and seeing miracles on the streets. Read this if you hunger for the supernatural and want to live dangerously for Jesus.

Che Ahn
President of Harvest International Ministry
Senior Pastor, Harvest Rock Church

Developing a Supernatural Lifestyle is a totally refreshing break from the countless "how to" prosper books which flood the mar-ket today. Rather, Kris Vallotton has given us both a menu and a roadmap to the gift of life God offers us in Christ Jesus. Some-how, somewhere, the church has lost sight of the biblical adven-ture of radical love and daring obedience, and has instead focused on religiously correct milquetoast conformity. Not only does Kris invite us to step out into the grand exploits of a Holy Spirit-led life, but he shares wisdom about the journey that is priceless.

Marc A. Dupont
Mantle of Praise Ministries, Inc.

Kris Vallotton has done us a powerful but painful favor. He has confronted us with the necessity of change from layer after layer of religion to the bringing of the supernatural life of Heaven into play in the earth. With many references to key

Scriptures and appropriate illustrations of personal supernatural occurrences, he makes his case unarguable. It is inevitable that when the last pages are read many will be asking, "Where have I been? Why hasn't somebody told me this before?" Supernatural living is not an option if the church is to touch the world, it is a mandate. Our choice seems clear. God is ready. Are we?

Jack Taylor
Dimensions Ministries
Melbourne, Florida

Developing a Supernatural Lifestyle will make you glad, mad, or sad. It will truly impact you and you will not be able to read it without a reaction and response! Personally, it made me very, very glad! I so resonate with its message. It is like a sword that pierces through the deep places of the soul exposing, sifting, and analyzing. This is an outstanding, outrageous book...a prophetic manuscript...an apostolic blueprint. Thanks, Kris, for your great courage to communicate mysteries that many are longing to understand.

Patricia King
Extreme Prophetic

In this persuasive book, Kris Vallotton encourages the Body of Christ to seek the supernatural gifts of the Spirit, offers training in their use, and incites us to change the world with them. You will be fascinated with his stories and intrigued by his insights. If you have longed to move in power or have been intimidated by the dark side, this book is for you! I recommend it for every serious Christian.

Pat Boone
Recording artist, movie star, and author

Developing a Supernatural Lifestyle clearly explains the gifts of the Holy Spirit and how to use them. He brings a greater clarity about how to prepare and expect prophetic dreams, visions, and experiences. He also teaches how to live a moral life and how to discern what is the Lord and what is not. You don't know what you can do until you stand up and try...then the Lord will honor your faith, show up, and show off!

Bob Jones
Itinerate minister and prophet

Developing a Supernatural Lifestyle is very encouraging to do just that—develop a supernatural lifestyle. His call for personal experience of God and with God are important corrections to a form of Christianity in the West that so frequently substitutes information for instruction, doctrines about God in place of the personal knowledge of God, and formulas in place of radical, risky faith. Kris presents a view of living in the Kingdom and in a Church that has been endowed with great beauty and power, a beautiful body that would be difficult to reject. He is not presenting a form of Christianity that is dogma and doctrine alone. He is not inviting people to come hug a skeleton.

Randy Clark
Global Awakening Apostolic Missions Network
Harrisburg, Pennsylvania

Table of Contents

❧

Foreword

One of the most amazing stories I have ever watched unfold has been the nearly 30-year-long journey of the author into a lifestyle of the supernatural. Kris and I have been friends for all that time, and partners in ministry for well over 20 years. His beginnings were the most humble imaginable. But there was a hunger and a willingness to serve that enabled him to rise both in experience and stature.

This journey began in Mountain Chapel of Weaverville, California. Day after day Kris would look for any possible place to serve. His passion for more of an authentic gospel caused him to grow in maturity, and eventually to a place of leadership. He stood out because of his relentless pursuit of a supernatural lifestyle as a normal part of the everyday Christian experience. While he was born with strong prophetic gifting, it was not yet functioning in any practical sense in the early stages of his quest. But that soon changed. And much of the breakthroughs we experienced in those years were in part due to Kris' gift.

After moving to Redding, California to pastor Bethel Church, I asked Kris to come and join my staff. He said yes and left the business world to do so. That was about 9 years ago. Some go to seminary or Bible College to get trained. But Kris went into the marketplace to do his learning as it was God's assignment for that season of his life. It would be in that environment that God would train Kris in the things he had hoped to learn in a school – the normal Christian life of miracles, signs and wonders. After joining our staff God added to Kris' schooling by exposing him to another world – church life. It was the combination of the two that God used to give him an extraordinary wisdom about the supernatural lifestyle both in and out of the church. What he teaches, he lives.

Kris' journey continues, as does mine. There is more available to anyone who will give themselves completely to displaying an authentic gospel. My heart is that you would give yourself to honoring our Lord Jesus Christ by displaying His love, character, and power. This book will go along way in making the *much desired supernatural lifestyle* a reality in your life. I highly recommend both the man and message, for they are one and the same.

Bill Johnson

Developing a Supernatural Lifestyle

In the days of the prophet Elijah, there arose a company of men who were called the *"sons of the prophets."* These men traveled throughout the world ravaging the powers of darkness and wreaking havoc on evil kingdoms. They had no tolerance for the destructive behavior of wicked kings but rather turned many to righteousness. They raised the dead, healed the sick, parted rivers, destroyed false prophets, and saw revival spread out through their land. They were feared by many and respected by all. They walked in great purity, and God was their friend.

Today, all around us, wickedness continues to grow, taking root in the lives of those we love and eroding the very foundation of our country. Satanism is spreading like wildfire. Psychics laugh in the face of the Church as they demonstrate the power of the dark side. Divorce is destroying our families and violence our children. Cancer, AIDS, other diseases take the lives of so many. Yet the words of our Lord Jesus echo through the halls of history: *"These signs will follow those who believe"* and *"Greater works than*

You are the bridge!

these [you] *will do, because I go to My Father"* (Mark 16:17; John 14:12 NKJV).

In Acts 3:25, Peter says, *"It is you who are the sons of the prophets."* It is time for the Body of Christ to rise up and receive our inheritance! We must rid ourselves of complacency and restore the ancient boundaries of holiness and demonstrations of great power. We cannot be satisfied with illustrated sermons, great music, and friendly services. We have been called to see the powers of darkness destroyed and our ruined cities restored.

In the days of Moses, God demonstrated His power to Pharaoh, but Pharaoh counter-attacked by having his sorcerers duplicate the miracles of God. Then the God of Heaven, who has all power, performed *extraordinary* miracles so that even the sorcerers said, "This must be God. We cannot perform these miracles." Finally Pharaoh was overcome by God's power and let His people go.

I believe that the Pharaoh of this world is about to let go of our cities as God demonstrates His raw, superior power through His Church. We are in the midst of the greatest revival in human history. Yet there remains a distance between what *should* be and what *will* be.

That distance is you!

What will *you* be?

You are the bridge between history and *His story*. You are the bridge!

You are *the sons of the prophets!*

The sick, the demonized, the poor, the blind, the lame and the lost are all waiting to see what you have learned.

Don't disappoint them!

CHAPTER 1

History Makers

Every so often in the course of history there are individuals born who defy common reason and statistical explanation. These are the great ones who break the tether of their generational expectations and rise to the high call that seems to echo from somewhere beyond the grave.

The prophets of old peered into the future and spoke of these violent ones who would force their way into the Kingdom, take hold of Heaven, and pull it down to earth. These reigning saints refuse to have their exploits be a mere reflection of the past, but instead break the gravitational barriers of naysayers and doubters, journeying far beyond the boundaries of reason into places where no one has ever gone before. Ultimately they capture the prize of the upward call of God that lies in Christ Jesus. These are God's history makers, the Lord's chosen people, His mighty men, His holy nation.

Many of us can feel the vacuum of this vortex drawing our hearts into this divine destiny. We find our inner man longing, stirring, and burning for the great adventure. Live or die, we must press through the walls of mediocrity and find the Promised Land of our souls. We live with a passion to be numbered among those who have gained fame in the halls of Heaven and are feared among the prison guards of hell. If we are going to walk as God's ruling royalty, it is incumbent upon us to:

- ✦ Pray unceasingly
- ✦ Give sacrificially.
- ✦ Dream unreasonably.
- ✦ Serve wholeheartedly.
- ✦ Love unashamedly.
- ✦ Walk innocently.
- ✦ Believe undoubtingly.
- ✦ Live powerfully.

These are the qualities of the Bride of Christ in all of her glory. She is called to be the most creative force on the face of the earth. Therefore we must not allow ourselves to become known for our boxes—that is, famous for what we don't do because of our righteous constrictions. Abraham Lincoln, George Washington, and Benjamin Franklin had certain moral values that restrained their behavior, but they were famous for what they did, not for what they didn't do! It would be tragic if the most creative people on the face of the earth allowed themselves to be reduced to rent-a-cops guarding a box (the Ark of the Covenant) that God vacated 2,000 years ago. Don't become famous for what you *don't* do.

> *Don't become famous for what you don't do.*
> ❦

The truth is that if we don't take our rightful place in the earth, we will relegate sinners, void of the mind of Christ, barred from the wisdom of the ages, and wandering in utter darkness, to being the most brilliant minds of our time! If the brightest light in this world belongs to those locked in darkness, how great would the darkness be in our world? Something is fundamentally wrong with this picture, but this is our brain on religion. Religion is like kryptonite to Superman. Religion can conform the most righteous, reigning saints into mindless zombies, puppets repeating someone else's convictions they don't even understand themselves.

Religion is like kryptonite to Superman.

ATTACK OF THE CLONES

I am convinced that religion is the father of genetic cloning. Religion invented cloning long before the world ever thought of it. Religion has a way of sucking the most powerful people on the planet into a spiritual look-a-like contest and calling it discipleship. True discipleship is meant to empower people to be transformed into the image of their Creator, but religion redefines the terms, conforming people into replicas of their leaders. Religion takes God's mighty men and makes them artifacts in a museum.

Religious people, like the Pharisees of old, have the hardest time reaching out to folks who think "outside of the box" and don't behave inside their hopeless shackles. Part of the struggle comes from what they have done to the Savior of the world. They have sterilized the gospel. Jesus took water and turned it to wine, but 2,000 years later today's Pharisees have diluted it to grape juice. Religion has reduced the supernatural power of God to a history lesson about serving the dead body of a helpless Christ who, still nailed to the Cross, is incapable of rocking their sacred boat. They emphasize the drowning of baptism, arguing over how people should get wet and what should be said over them during their dipping. Religious people have lost touch with the fact that the bold print of baptism is not on the descent but on the ascension. The death of Christ paid for our sins, but it was His resurrection that gave life to our mortal bodies.

Religion embraces death sadistically and moves the risen Christ out of the garden and back to the tomb. Religious people pray things like "God, kill me," not realizing that even the One who came to give His life as a ransom for us all, prayed *"Father, if You are willing, remove this cup* [of death] *from Me; yet not My will, but Yours be done"* (Luke 22:42). Jesus did not want to die; He wanted to do His Father's will. If religion had its way it would rewrite Mary's proclamation to read, "He is in the tomb just where we laid Him!" We have lost sight of the fact that the Cross was for the old man, not the new man, and that the true Christian life is not about dying for Christ, but living in the life He purchased for us to establish His Kingdom on earth! The Church must shake off the shackles of religion and embrace our supernatural destiny. The Cross was for the old man—not the new man.

OUR COMMISSION

The world is crying out in distress, and we must not miss this *kairos* moment, the opportunity of the ages. In the late sixties, the Beatles took America by storm. In a few short years, four boys from Liverpool altered the course of our nation's history. Soon after, the world was swept into the wake of their anointing—all while they were singing "Yeah, yeah, yeah." But it wasn't long before the "Fab Four" started to experience a crisis in their own souls. They began to cry out in desperation, singing:

> *The Cross was for the old man—not the new man.*

(Help) I need somebody
(Help) Not just anybody
(Help) You know I need someone

(Help)

24

When I was younger, so much younger than today,
I never needed anybody's help in any way.
But now these days are gone

I'm not so self-assured
Now I find I've changed my mind
I've opened up the doors.

Help me if you can, I'm feeling down
And I do appreciate you being 'round.

Help me get my feet back on the ground
Won't you please, please help me!

http://www.thebeatles.com.hk/lyrics/lyrics.asp?ly
Title=Help%21+%28Love+version%29

© 1995-2007 The Beatles Studio,
www.thebeatles.com.hk;

But their cry for help fell on deaf ears in the sanctuary of hope, and soon they were calling Hare Krishna their "sweet lord." The Church can't afford to fall asleep in the harvest today as we have done so many times in the past. We are not supposed to reflect our culture; we are commissioned to transform it.

We are called to disciple all the nations of the world. Discipling nations means submerging them in God—not religion—and *"teaching them to observe all that I commanded you"* (Matt. 28:20). Teaching nations how to think is the transformational catalyst to changing cultures. But as long as Christians aren't valued in society they will have no influence in the world. (You only have as much influence in people's lives as they have value for you. Anytime you try to have more influence than someone has value for you, you will manipulate them.)

> *Christians must be valued in society to have influence in the world.*

Christians must be valued in society to have influence in the world.

It is imperative that we become kings who understand the ways that royal people influence authority. Otherwise we will reduce ourselves to social begging, hoping that the *big*, powerful people feel compassion for us and help our cause. This poisonous poverty mind-set reduces the Christian message to a cry for help instead of a call for leadership. We don't need nations to change for our sake. We have a living, abiding, unshakable Kingdom that dwells within us and prospers under all circumstances. We need the nations to change for the sake of those still lost in darkness. They need the culture around them to create a safe environment for them until they get the Kingdom within them.

This cultural begging has relegated the Kingdom of God to a subculture. God never intended Christianity to be a subculture. Subcultures are those cultures that are subservient to a more powerful culture. The world's commentary on the first-century Church reflects the true influence we are meant to have in society. They proclaimed, *"These who have turned the world upside down have come here too"* (Acts 17:6 NKJV). We are called to turn the world around and set it back on its feet again. We are to be counter-culture until the mind-set of the nations begins to take on the attitude of the Kingdom. Christians are not subservient to the world because God has assigned us the highest level of authority that exists on this planet. God never intended Christianity to be a subculture.

> *God never intended Christianity to be a subculture.*

When Christians lose their desire and courage to confront the evils of our day honorably, we begin to be influenced by the lying principalities that are also commissioned to disciple the nations, but with an antichrist agenda. These demonic forces work to dethrone the Prince of Peace, who is the rightful "prince" of the principles that make societies prosper, and instead enthrone the prince of darkness. Consequently, the enabling principles of a culture become demonically inspired instead of Kingdom in-Spirited. This dark prince works to establish evil thinking that leads to destructive behaviors. But when Jesus rules, He enables the principles of the King to transform the culture through the mind of Christ. In other words, people in a nation governed by the Kingdom begin to think like God!

However, it is important that we learn how to carry His power and authority. If we believers become combative instead of honorably confronting, we will reduce our influence to the small pond of the church and render ourselves powerless in the ocean of humanity. We are to carry God's authority into the lives of people and nations through invitation, not through intrusion or invasion. Although we are called to be combative when dealing with the powers of darkness, we are to be honorably confronting with people, demonstrating the benefits and rewards of a superior Kingdom.

TEARING DOWN FORTRESSES

Daniel had a vision of the Last Days that sheds light on the point I am addressing here. He wrote:

> [The devil] *will speak out against the Most High and wear down the saints of the Highest One, and he will intend to* **make alterations in times and in law;** *and they will be given into his hand for a time, times, and half a time. But the court will sit for judgment, and his dominion will be taken away, annihilated and destroyed forever. Then the sovereignty, the dominion and the greatness of all the kingdoms under the whole heaven will be given to the people of the saints of the Highest One; His kingdom will be an everlasting kingdom, and all the dominions will serve and obey Him* (Daniel 7:25-27).

Daniel saw the devil apprehending the "times" or epoch seasons and changing the law. These epoch seasons or "times" are similar to the time periods we call the agricultural age, the industrial age, and the information age. Halfway through the third epoch, God stripped authority from the devil and gave it to the saints. The devil tried to alter the times by changing the law. The law mentioned here is not the Torah, but the decrees and the rules of society. Changes in the law are signs of the times and manifestations of the new value systems of mankind in a particular epoch. Epoch seasons are altered when people begin to think differently and develop structures to sustain their new and emerging attitudes.

These structures are built inside of people before they ever emerge as decrees and rules in the society around them. These internal structures are constructed through demonically inspired "in-struction" that has shaped their souls. Paul teaches us about this in Second Corinthians. He writes:

> *For though we walk in the flesh, we do not war according to the flesh, for the weapons of our warfare are not of the flesh, but divinely powerful for the destruction of fortresses. We are destroying speculations and every lofty thing raised up against the knowledge of God, and we are taking every thought captive to the obedience of Christ* (2 Corinthians 10:3-5).

Paul describes fortresses as *speculations, lofty things,* and *thoughts.* Fortresses are systems of firmly held wrong beliefs that

Evil spirits are the ultimate body snatchers.

squeeze the life of God out of the hearts of people, changing the culture in a way that ultimately hijacks the divine destiny of nations themselves. These fortresses are assembled brick by brick through the intentional *in-struction* of demonic *speculations*—such speculations as, "There is no Creator. Life transpired through a big bang." Or how about this one: "A fetus is not a baby; it is just tissue until it emerges from the mother's womb. Then it suddenly becomes a human being." *Lofty things*, or arrogant attitudes, are seen in statements such as, "Man is god and there is no one to whom he needs to submit." *Thoughts* can be many things, but every thought is an interpretation of reality, and thus is connected to a belief system based either on truth or lies. Wrong thoughts undermine the love of the Bridegroom and ultimately produce behavior that denies who we are, since we were made in the image of our loving Creator. Evil spirits are the ultimate body snatchers.

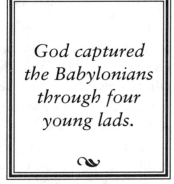

God captured the Babylonians through four young lads.

The great news is that God is calling His Church to develop a supernatural lifestyle that equips the saints of the Most High with weapons of warfare that are not of the flesh but that are divinely powerful, supernaturally inspired arsenals of mass destruction! Under the cover of darkness, the Lord has been distributing these weapons of light to prepare us for a mass invasion against the evil forces that have hidden out in the hearts of men. These evil spirits are the ultimate body snatchers. But Heaven is invading earth, freeing captives and releasing prisoners.

In the days of Daniel, Nebuchadnezzar destroyed Israel and took Daniel and his three friends captive. But the Babylonians underestimated the "X factor." Like the superheroes in an action movie, these boys began supernaturally and systematically to dismantle the wicked systems of ancient Iraq from the inside. Nebuchadnezzar thought that he had captured four young Jewish lads, but it was the Babylonians who were taken prisoner by the God of Heaven. Over the next 70 years these men escaped the furnace, turned lions into pussycats, and changed the nation's history through prophetic proclamations and dream interpretations. God captured the Babylonians through four young lads.

TRAINING FOR THE WORLD

Unlike the ministry of Daniel, much of the supernatural ministry in the new millennium reminds me of the four-wheel-drive vehicles in the big city where I grew up. It was cool to own a four-wheel-drive truck in the Bay Area, and guys would buy these trucks, jack them way up in the air, put on huge tires and a triple roll bar, and dress them in chrome. Years later we moved way up in the mountains of the Trinity Alps. One of the first things I noticed was that nobody had jacked up, chromed out trucks. Most of these mountain folks owned rugged-looking four-wheel-drives with beat-up paint jobs and narrow tires that could bite in the snow, because they used them to get in and out of the woods in the middle of the winter. They didn't own them to perpetuate their image. These trucks were just pieces of equipment the mountain folks needed to live.

God never intended the gifts of the Spirit to be confined to the four walls of the Church. Most of the miracles in the Bible took place off the holy highway in the rugged backwoods of the marketplace. Thankfully, there is a great transition happening in the Kingdom. We are moving from the ministry *to* the saints to the ministry *of* the saints. Church is the place where we go to get equipped with the *weapons of warfare*, and it is a great place to practice until we get proficient with them, under the guidance of experienced instructors. But it is important to equip, develop, and train with deployment in mind.

The previous war in Iraq is a great example of this. In Desert Storm the United States military found itself ill prepared for the battle. Our tanks, helicopters, and guns filled up with sand and broke down. Our camouflaged uniforms stuck out like a sore thumb in the sands of Iraq and our troops were not prepared for the incredible heat and sandstorms that plagued them in the desert. One of the main problems could be traced back to the fact that our troops had been prepared with the jungles of Vietnam in mind. The desert of Iraq was a far cry from the tropical challenges of jungle warfare. But by the time the second Iraq War began, America was ready because our troops had been equipped and trained with that particular battlefield in sight. Training with pussycats won't prepare you for the lion's den.

> *Training with pussycats won't prepare you for the lion's den.*
>
> ∽

Most Christians are not prepared for the battle that awaits them in the marketplace because they have trained in the user-friendly environment of "Fort Cush." Not only were they trained *among* nice people who already know God and speak Christianese, they have *trained for them!* It is hard to be prepared for the lion's den while training with and for pussycats.

Let me make it clear; the church should be a safe place to practice and grow in the Holy Spirit's gifts. But if we train only *for the Church* we will be completely ineffective among those lost in darkness. You can only sit in the simulator so long before you finally have to go out and take a drive in the real thing.

I remember when our youngest son, Jason, first learned to shoot a bow and arrow. We lived in the woods, so we set up a target for him on some bales of hay behind our house. He was five years old when we bought him his first compound bow. He would go out in the backyard and shoot that thing for hours. Then one day I noticed that when he picked up the bow to go outside, our dog cowered and ran out the door the other way. You can only practice for so long before you start getting the urge to try your skill on something that's living.

At Bethel School of Supernatural Ministry we train our students with the marketplace in mind. For instance, when they are learning to minister in the word of knowledge or prophecy we try to simulate the place of deployment as much as possible. The students match up one-on-one. They are then instructed to ask the Holy Spirit for a word of knowledge or prophecy for their partner in 30 seconds. There is no music playing in the background and they have to try even if they get it wrong. They are to deliver the message in conversational English, not yelling, shaking, dramatizing the word or using King James language.

Why do we require them to practice like this? Because you won't typically have a beautiful song playing in the background when you minister at the mall. We only give them 30 seconds so they get used to getting a word quickly and don't miss opportunities in the marketplace. They deliver the word in plain, conversational English so that people in the world can relate to them. We also have them judge each other's ministry to determine if it was from God and if it was delivered accurately. We tell them, "Turn off your mercy gift when you are giving your partner feedback. They need an honest analysis of their ministry, not flattery." When the students start gaining experience and begin to get pretty accurate, we send them, accompanied by a mature leader, into the marketplace, the streets, and the schools to minister to real people. When they return, we debrief with them so they can gain insight into how to become more effective.

Like the Bethel School of Supernatural Ministry, this book is dedicated to developing revivalists who make history. My prayer is that these revivalists become:

- ✧ Humble, but not harmless
- ✧ Honorable, but not suck-ups
- ✧ Dependable, but not predictable
- ✧ Bold, but not brash
- ✧ Holy, but not hobbled
- ✧ Patient, but not passive
- ✧ Powerful, but not controlling
- ✧ Encouraging, without flattering
- ✧ Gentle, but not timid

✧ Modest, but not docile

✧ Confident, but not cocky

✧ Steadfast, but not stubborn

✧ Teachable, but not tame

✧ Kind, but not benign

✧ Discerning, but not suspicious

✧ Confrontational, but not combative

✧ Tough, but not rigid

✧ Submissive, but not subdued

✧ Serious, but not somber

✧ Risky, yet wise

✧ Peaceful, but not careless

✧ Spontaneous, yet prepared

✧ Giving, yet able to receive

✧ Transparent, but able to keep a secret

✧ Extreme, yet balanced

✧ Spirit-led, but self-controlled

✧ Submitted to men, but following God.

If your heart burns to be famous in Heaven and known in hell and if you have the courage to read on, I will meet you in the pages of this book.

CHAPTER 2

Victims, Vampires, and Voices

‍❧

In the projects where I grew up there was a canal down the street from my house. One day my friend Ray and I decided to build a boat to float the "river." We went to my house and found some plywood lying around in my backyard. We cut a boat shape out of a large piece of plywood and then nailed some sides to it. It looked pretty cool and we were very proud of it. Ray and I carried the thing down to the canal and lifted it over the fence. We could hardly wait to put her in the water and jump in. We slid her into the river, but to our utter amazement she began to sink. There was a large knot in the plywood bottom that had fallen out, and water came pouring into the boat. (I am sure it was leaking in a hundred other places too, but those leaks seemed insignificant.) With a ton of effort we rescued our boat from the bottom of the "sea." Then we took her back to the shop for some emergency repairs.

In the midst of our ship repair my stepfather came out of the house and took a look at our progress. We were just beginning to use a large hole-saw to drill another hole in the bottom of the hull.

"What are you doing?" he asked with a chuckle.

"We have water coming through that knothole in the bottom of the boat, so we are going to drill another hole in the hull the same size as the knothole so that the water can drain back out the other hole," I answered.

"Oh!" he replied. "That makes great sense." We couldn't figure out why he was laughing so hard as he walked away.

We carried our boat back to the canal and lifted it over the fence to commence her maiden voyage. But we were again shocked when we put her in the water. Water poured in from both holes! Our little boat went the way of the Titanic and sank to the bottom of the ocean.

My friend and I were ignorant of a few simple principles that ultimately led to a sinking ship. This reminds me so much of the Church. Paul said, *"Now concerning spiritual gifts, brethren, I do not want you to be unaware"* (1 Cor. 12:1). The word "gifts" in this verse is not in the original text. It actually reads, "Now concerning the spiritual, brethren, I don't want you to be unaware." So much of the Church is ignorant of the spirit world. The result is that many people have become victims of the cults while trying to find answers to their spiritual encounters. Many Christians do not have a clue how the spirit realm works or how its influence affects them. Consequently, these people often get the lifeblood sucked out of them because they have become victims of the invisible.

MESHA'S BIRDS

The members of my family have experienced the spirit realm firsthand many times. My granddaughter Mesha is no exception. When Mesha was 18 months old she began behaving rather strangely. Jaime, my daughter, would go into her room and find her talking and interacting with someone who was invisible. Mesha called these invisible people "birds." At first we all thought this was just the normal "kid pretending" thing. But something about these "birds" troubled us, although we couldn't put our finger on it. Mesha seemed to know things that she said the "birds" told her. One day Jaime was taking a bath with Mesha. The presence of the Lord suddenly filled the bathroom in such a powerful way that it startled my daughter. They both sat up in the tub and Mesha shouted, "The birds are here!" She

Our spirit takes us to places our minds would never go!

began to giggle and laugh as she interacted with them. Jaime immediately realized that these "birds" that Mesha had been talking about for months were actually angels! Our spirit takes us to places our minds would never go!

As Mesha has gotten older (she is eight years old at the writing of this book), these encounters have grown stronger and more profound. The angel that comes to visit her most often told Mesha that "her" name was Beniah. Beniah would often come dressed in different colors like gold, purple, and red, which seemed to mean something to Mesha. Mesha speaks of the angels as one would speak of a close friend.

Recently Mesha called me on the phone as she often does. I asked her if she had seen Beniah lately. "No," she replied. "She's on a 'time out' because she disobeyed God." Wow! Could that be true? I really don't know. But I've learned that much of the Kingdom lies in the realm of mystery. Bill Johnson put it like this, "If you understand everything that happens to you in the Kingdom, than you have an inferior Christian experience because so much of our life in God is veiled in mystery." Our spirit can take us places our minds would never go!

Once Mesha was putting on her shoes, getting ready for school, when her mom walked into her room. She looked up and said, "Mom, Jesus has been taking me to Heaven a lot lately." She went on to tell Jaime that she had been to Heaven 14 times in 14 days.

Jaime asked her if she was having dreams of Heaven. "Nope," she replied. "I have visions."

Jaime said, "Are you seeing these visions with your mind?"

"No, Mom. I see them with my eyes." Then Mesha went on to describe Heaven in great detail. She said, "Heaven is a very beautiful place and someday I am going to live there."

Jaime asked her if Jesus talks to her. "Yes," she replied. "He told me that He has a lot for me to do!"

Mesha may seem super-spiritual to you but most of the time she is just a normal little girl who loves to have fun. When people like Mesha have encounters with the spirit realm and don't understand what has happened to them, they often look for counsel at their local church. The struggle is that many leaders in the Body of Christ simply don't understand much about the invisible realm, or they often don't really believe in it at all. As a result, they give advice like, "You need to see a psychiatrist," or "You need to read the Bible more, come to church more often, and spend more time in prayer." Some of these things can certainly be true for people, but these pat answers don't solve most people's longing for insight into their supernatural encounters. To further compound the problem, if the people who are having these encounters happen to share their story with someone in the occult or Wicca, a New Age person, a psychic, or a Buddhist, they will usually find that these people understand them and have had similar encounters!

For some Christians the fact that people who aren't believers have similar spiritual experiences indicates that *all* these encounters are from the dark side and must be repented of. This is simply not true. Spiritual encounters are common throughout the entire Bible. Trances, angelic visitations, visions, third heaven experiences, exorcisms, and loads of other spiritual phenomena are talked about in the Old and New Testament. It is true that many of these encounters are from the dark side, but that doesn't change the fact that the Kingdom of God is a spiritual experience.

God is often the One who initiates these manifestations. Where do you think the devil got the idea for this stuff? He is not a creator—only a copycat.

Here are a few examples of supernatural encounters that people in the Bible had with the spirit world. I will explore some of these in greater detail later in the book.

TRANCES

Here is Luke's account of a trance that Peter had. This led to the conversion of the first Gentile family.

> *On the next day, as they were on their way and approaching the city, Peter went up on the housetop about the sixth hour to pray. But he became hungry and was desiring to eat; but while they were making preparations, he fell into a trance; and he saw the sky opened up, and an object like a great sheet coming down, lowered by four corners to the ground, and there were in it all kinds of four-footed animals and crawling creatures of the earth and birds of the air. A voice came to him, "Get up, Peter, kill and eat!" But Peter said, "By no means, Lord, for I have never eaten anything unholy and unclean." Again a voice came to him a second time, "What God has cleansed, no longer consider unholy." This happened three times, and immediately the object was taken up into the sky* (Acts 10:9-16).

PEOPLE FLYING THROUGH THE AIR

Here is a strange spiritual experience that Ezekiel had. I bet all of us would be a little surprised to see a hand grab our pastor and take him flying through midair.

> *It came about in the sixth year, on the fifth day of the sixth month, as I was sitting in my house with the elders of Judah sitting before me, that the hand of the Lord God fell on me there. Then I looked, and behold, a likeness as the appearance of a man; from His loins and downward there*

*was the appearance of fire, and from His loins and up-
ward the appearance of brightness, like the appearance of
glowing metal. He stretched out the form of a hand and
caught me by a lock of my head; and the Spirit lifted me up
between earth and heaven and brought me in the visions
of God to Jerusalem, to the entrance of the north gate of the
inner court, where the seat of the idol of jealousy, which
provokes to jealousy, was located* (Ezekiel 8:1-3).

DEAD PEOPLE RETURN

How would you like to go to the downtown mall and meet
King David or run into Queen Esther at Wendy's? Well, that is exactly what happened in this next story.

*The tombs were opened, and many bodies of the saints who
had fallen asleep were raised; and coming out of the tombs
after His resurrection they entered the holy city and appeared to many* (Matthew 27:52-53).

Here is a similarly strange experience that Jesus had with three
of His disciples. They went up on a mountain, where Jesus started
glowing (this is before His resurrection), after which two dead
saints showed up and start talking to Him. If that's not weird
enough, a voice started yelling from Heaven! The whole experience scared the bejeebers out of the disciples.

*Six days later, Jesus took with Him Peter and James and
John, and brought them up on a high mountain by
themselves. And He was transfigured before them; and
His garments became radiant and exceedingly white, as
no launderer on earth can whiten them. Elijah appeared
to them along with Moses; and they were talking with
Jesus. Peter said to Jesus, "Rabbi, it is good for us to be
here; let us make three tabernacles, one for You, and one
for Moses, and one for Elijah." For he did not know what
to answer; for they became terrified. Then a cloud formed,*

overshadowing them, and a voice came out of the cloud,
"This is My beloved Son, listen to Him!" (Mark 9:2-7)

ANGELIC VISITATIONS

Angels were a major part of life in the early Church. Angels are mentioned more than 190 times in the New Testament alone. The Holy Spirit is only mentioned 27 more times than angels in the New Testament. I am not saying that angels are as important as God Himself; I am simply pointing out that people in the New Testament experienced them nearly as often.

God sent an angel to save Joseph's marriage to Mary, the mother of Jesus.

> *Now the birth of Jesus Christ was as follows: when His mother Mary had been betrothed to Joseph, before they came together she was found to be with child by the Holy Spirit. And Joseph her husband, being a righteous man and not wanting to disgrace her, planned to send her away secretly. But when he had considered this, behold, an angel of the Lord appeared to him in a dream, saying, "Joseph, son of David, do not be afraid to take Mary as your wife; for the Child who has been conceived in her is of the Holy Spirit* (Matthew 1:18-20).

Here is a wild story about an angel performing a jailbreak on Herod's high security prison. He springs Peter by leading him right out the front gate. I wonder what we would think if someone came to our church and told us that an angel just broke them out of San Quentin!

> *Now about that time Herod the king laid hands on some who belonged to the church in order to mistreat them. And he had James the brother of John put to death with a sword. When he saw that it pleased the Jews, he proceeded to arrest Peter also. Now it was during the days of Unleavened Bread. When he had seized him, he put him in prison, delivering him to four*

squads of soldiers to guard him, intending after the Passover to bring him out before the people. So Peter was kept in the prison, but prayer for him was being made fervently by the church to God. On the very night when Herod was about to bring him forward, Peter was sleeping between two soldiers, bound with two chains, and guards in front of the door were watching over the prison. And behold, an angel of the Lord suddenly appeared and a light shone in the cell; and he struck Peter's side and woke him up, saying, "Get up quickly." And his chains fell off his hands. And the angel said to him, "Gird yourself and put on your sandals." And he did so. And he said to him, "Wrap your cloak around you and follow me." And he went out and continued to follow, and he did not know that what was being done by the angel was real, but thought he was seeing a vision. When they had passed the first and second guard, they came to the iron gate that leads into the city, which opened for them by itself; and they went out and went along one street, and immediately the angel departed from him (Acts 12:1-10).

The Church's response to Peter's release is quite revealing. When he came to the house where they were praying for him to be released, the people thought it was an angel and refused to believe it was him. Angel sightings must have been very common, because it took less faith to believe that there was an angel at the door, taking on the likeness of Peter, than it did to believe that God had answered their prayers!

When Peter came to himself, he said, "Now I know for sure that the Lord has sent forth His angel and rescued me from the hand of Herod and from all that the Jewish people were expecting." And when he realized this, he went to the house of Mary, the mother of John who was also called Mark, where many were gathered together and were praying. When he knocked at the door of the gate, a servant-girl named Rhoda came to answer. When she recognized

Peter's voice, because of her joy she did not open the gate, but ran in and announced that Peter was standing in front of the gate. They said to her, "You are out of your mind!" But she kept insisting that it was so. They kept saying, "It is his angel." But Peter continued knocking; and when they had opened the door, they saw him and were amazed (Acts 12:11-16).

God intends His people to be the best army ever.

WE NEED TO KNOW WHAT'S BEHIND THE DOOR

Church leaders often disarm Christians who walk in these manifestations because they see the same things in the cults or the occult. They produce ill-equipped believers who, instead of casting out demonic spirits, futilely try to preach them into powerlessness, which simply allows these spirits to continue tormenting the world. God intended for His people to be the finest, best-equipped, best-trained army that ever graced this planet. But the lack of understanding among Christians has created a spiritual vacuum in the world that has allowed the cults and the occult to grow like crazy. They have become the unpaid bills of the Church, and they must be stopped! God intends His people to be the best army ever.

The world is starving for spiritual understanding. This *should* be a historic time in the Church, the high point of the ages. Look at the movies that have come out of Hollywood in the last 20 years. From *The Exorcist* to Harry Potter, people are fascinated with the spirit realm. But instead of seizing the day, many Christians are getting run over by evil spirits who are propagating their garbage to our families through cultic dissemination. We must rise up in this hour and come to the forefront of spiritual understanding so that we can lead this nation out of darkness and into the light.

Don't become an invisible man casualty.

King Solomon said, "Knowledge is easy to one who has understanding" (Prov. 14:6b). Understanding the heart of God, the realm of the invisible, and the responsibility and authority we have in Christ releases the key of knowledge to us.

Here is an example that drives home the point I am trying to make. A while back I walked by our recording studio at Bethel Church and was drawn to a sign that has been on the door for years. It reads, "Stop Nursing Mothers Only." The music studio doubles as a room for nursing mothers on Sundays. Suddenly I got this revelation: If you were unaware that the studio was also a nursing room for mothers, you couldn't understand the sign. I began to think about the possible messages that the sign could imply to those who were ignorant of the room's multiple uses. Could it mean, "Only stop nursing mothers. Everyone else can go beyond this point"? Or how about this one: "We must stop mothers from nursing." Or could it indicate something like, "Everyone can nurse except for mothers"? Of course these definitions sound silly to all of those who understand what is going on in that room on the weekends. We know the sign is actually not for nursing mothers at all. It is actually written to everyone else. It is obviously supposed to mean, "Don't come in here, because there are mothers nursing their babies!"

Likewise, in order for us to comprehend what is actually taking place in these supernatural encounters, we have to understand what is going on behind the veil of the visible. Much like the studio example, when we don't understand how the spirit realm functions, we come up with the strangest interpretations of these experiences. Unless we peer into the age to come we will become casualties of the invisible man. Don't become an invisible man casualty.

This mandate has become the mission for this manuscript. This book is dedicated to the unfolding mysteries of the Kingdom of

God that lie in the realm that is invisible to most of us, in order to equip the saints with spiritual gifts and to train them to build strategic alliances with heavenly allies. It is my heart's cry that this book would lead the Body of Christ to victories never before heard of or experienced in the history of the world, ultimately bringing *heaven* to *earth*.

CHAPTER 3

Life in the Kingdom Is a
Bunch of Bull

❧

Kathy and I got married in 1977. A couple years later we moved to Weaverville, a mountain community of about 3,000 people nestled in the Trinity Alps in Northern California. We bought a Union 76 service station in town that became our first Kingdom training center. The people in the community affectionately called us the "God Squad."

One January day it was snowing like crazy in the mountains where we lived and our town was about three feet deep in snow. It was so cold that day that we closed the bay doors and had the heater blowing full blast. The crew was working on cars and I was in the office doing the books. Sitting at my desk I had a beautiful view of the town through the large plate-glass windows surrounding the office. The wind was howling through the pump island, making the snow fall nearly horizontally.

At one point I looked out on the far pump island and saw, to my surprise, that a cow was standing on the driveway. I immediately noticed that the animal had a rope around its neck with a bell hanging from it. I called out to Dan, our pump island attendant, and advised him of the situation. *It's too cold to go out there myself,* I reasoned. *I am the boss! This is what I pay people to do...sort of.*

Dan went out for a closer look and then came running into the station yelling, "That is no cow—that's a bull!" The entire crew came to the shop window, laughing at Dan as he entered the shop in hysteria.

"Dan, go grab that rope and lead that animal off the pump island!" I demanded in the most authoritative tone I could muster.

"No way!" he shouted back, "You don't pay me enough to wrestle bulls. I'm not going back out there until that thing is gone!" I guess the bull had snorted at him when he got close to it.

"Look," I reasoned, "that bull is someone's pet. It's got a leash and a bell around its neck. What's the big deal?" I turned to the crew. "All right, men. Who is going to lead that bull off of our pump island?"

"Not me!" they said one by one.

"Fine. I'll do it myself!"

I was actually a little nervous about the whole thing. I moved slowly towards the bull, making sure of my exit in the event of an emergency. As I got closer I saw that the animal looked docile, almost friendly. I took a hold of the rope and gave it a little tug. The bull just grunted. So I jerked the rope harder and yelled, "Come on, Bull. Move those doggies!" This was something I learned on an old western. But that stubborn sucker wouldn't move.

I wrapped the rope several times around my hand to get a good grip and leaned into the bull. Just as I began to tug, the bull took off running. The stupid thing ran down the highway, against traffic. I couldn't let go of the rope because it had tightened around my hand. I had my snow boots on, and the bull was pulling me through the snow like a water skier behind a jet boat. The traffic stopped, and people were yelling and clapping as we passed them going the wrong way down the road. By now my crew was standing on the sidewalk cheering (for the bull, I think). I struggled to loose my hand, but the tension on the rope was too much. I started to run with the bull to try to take the strain off the rope.

Finally I managed to get free. I looked ahead and spotted a stop sign at the end of the block. I ran to the stop sign and wrapped the rope around the pole. The bull abruptly came to the end of the rope, bending the stop sign to the ground. Then he snorted, grunted, and turned towards me. I took off running back to the service station. With a jerk, the bull freed himself and took off after me. I could hear him snorting, right on my tail. When I got to the station my men were running for cover. I jumped on the wall that divided the station from the restaurant next door. The bull made one last attempt to gore me with his horns, but he missed. I now stood on the wall, safe at last. After about 15 minutes he finally lost interest and wandered away.

THE LAMB IS ALSO A LION

This story reminds me so much of the Kingdom of God. When we first come into the Kingdom it looks friendly, almost docile. Much like a cow, it seems like we can control and guide the Kingdom to meet our demands and fulfill our every want. Then we tie our hands of service to the Lord, and the bull takes off running. The Lamb suddenly turns into the Lion. Instead of taking it for a walk, it is dragging us through life. To make matters worse, all the people we know and who used to respect us, are watching us go down the *high-way* the wrong direction. To complicate the situation, this Bull/Lion is invisible to most folks, so we look ridiculous! When we finally develop some doctrines to get the animal stopped and our hope for normality begins to return, the bull frees itself, turns around, and begins to chase us back down the *high-way* of life.

> *Develop a pooper-scooper ministry to grow in the ministry of the Spirit.*
>
> ✍

My point is really simple: Life in the Kingdom is risky and messy. If you want to have a nice, neat, organized life, you will eliminate most of the works of God from your life. Proverbs puts it like this, *"Where no oxen are, the manger is clean, but much revenue comes by the strength of the ox"* (Prov. 14:4). Everyone knows what's in the manger when the oxen are there. Anytime we have real Holy Spirit ministry there will be a mess! When churches create enough rules to keep anything that can go wrong from happening in their services, the place becomes a museum, a monument to something that once was alive. Little takes place in the Spirit realm without taking a risk. I tell people that in order to grow in the ministry of the Spirit you must develop a pooper-scooper ministry along with it. Develop a pooper-scooper ministry to grow in the ministry of the Spirit.

DECENTLY AND IN ORDER

There are many people who quote Paul's exhortation to the Corinthians to justify their controlling culture. He said, *"Therefore, my brethren, desire earnestly to prophesy, and do not forbid to speak in tongues. But all things must be done properly and in an orderly manner"* (1 Cor. 14:39-40). There are several points that are often overlooked here. First, Paul says, *"All things must be done."* You have to have something going on before you concern yourself with putting it in order. Paul is writing to people who are zealous for spiritual gifts, and he is helping to bring order to the *Spirit life* that is *already happening* in their lives. You need not concern yourself with the teaching on order if you haven't got the "all things must be done" part. I have heard many church leaders teach on order who don't have anything going on to make orderly.

Fear will keep you from moving with the Spirit. Fear has many faces and it often masquerades as wisdom, dignity, or love. But underneath that mask is a scared believer who doesn't want to look bad. Bill Johnson says, "The Holy Spirit is imprisoned in the bodies of unbelieving believers." (I talked about this a lot more in my book *The Supernatural Ways of Royalty*.) The Holy Spirit is imprisoned in unbelieving believers' bodies.

Secondly, God's idea of order is completely different from ours. Romans says that we can learn how God thinks about life from observing nature itself. It reads, *"For since the creation of the world His invisible attributes, His eternal power and divine nature, have been clearly seen, being understood through what has been made, so that they are without excuse"* (Rom. 1:20).

This point was driven home to me when we had our first child. We were young and we had just been married a couple of years when Kathy gave birth to our daughter, Jaime. Before the birth Kathy convinced me to go to Lamaze classes to "help" her with the delivery. Lamaze is based around the concept of coaching a woman through the delivery process. I was to be Kathy's coach and assist her through the labor. The day she went into labor I figured out that the class was really a secret ploy to get husbands to suffer with their wives for getting them pregnant. Misery loves company. I now know that the word "Lamaze" is an ancient Hebrew word that means, "Hey stupid, how did you get in here?!"

Part of the secret ploy is to make you believe that when your wife is having contractions, you can actually help her by developing a focal point in the room and having her focus on it while you "coach" her breathing during the labor pains. I chose a Snickers Bar as a focal point for her because I thought we could both think about it together while she screamed bloody murder. Kathy had 28 hours of hard labor with Jaime. By the fifth hour I had already eaten the focal point! I'm not sure if it was her screaming or her accusing me of causing her all this pain

> *The Holy Spirit is imprisoned in unbelieving believers' bodies.*
>
> ❧

that bothered me the most. But the Lamaze scam was exposed as a fraud and like a house of cards, it crumbled under the pressure of a real delivery.

In spite of all this the big moment finally came. The baby decided to give up fighting for its home and meet the new world. Meanwhile, however, the sight of blood was difficult for me and I kept passing out. The doctor thought that it was his duty to keep me conscious so he continued waking me with smelling salts. Just when the whole thing got really ugly, Jaime's head popped out. Jaime didn't seem any happier about the whole thing than I was.

The doctor, trying to look calm, asked me if I wanted to cut the cord. I looked at him and said, "What did we pay you for?" (Man, that made me mad!)

After the cord was cut, the nurse tried to hand me this big, ol' bloody mess. "No way!" I responded. "I waited nine months for this; I can wait 15 minutes while you clean her up!" It was all very gross and even describing it makes me want to puke.

To make matters worse, the baby looked like she had been in a terrible car accident, and when my mom saw her she said in glee, "She looks just like you!"

Wow! Talk about a blow to my self-esteem. I looked in the mirror a hundred times a day for months after that! In spite of my trauma, I had to come to terms with the fact that my daughter's birth, along with many other ordinary processes that God ordained in creation and in His ministry, may not be "clean and tidy" yet they are what He calls "decently and in order."

LEARNING TO FAIL

Faith requires risk. If you never fail, you haven't really taken a risk. The word *risk* means, "You place something valued in a position or situation where it can be damaged, lost, or exposed to danger" (Encarta World English Dictionary). Risk is one of the main catalysts to a supernatural lifestyle. On the first day of each year at the Bethel Supernatural School of Ministry, I tell our students that if they don't fail at least three times during the school year they can't graduate. (Of course I am not talking about moral failure and I make that very clear.) We need to learn to fail successfully.

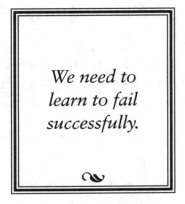

We need to learn to fail successfully.

We need to learn to fail successfully. When I taught my children to ride their bikes, I took them over to the lawn so that when—not if—they fell, they wouldn't get hurt. We need to develop a culture where trying and failing is viewed as success.

This point was driven home to me a few years ago. I met a great leader, whom I'll call "John," who had planted a church that had grown to several thousand people over a short period of time. We talked for a while over lunch, but I sensed that he was discouraged. I finally asked him what was bothering him. His eyes welled up with tears as he began to tell me the story of one of his best friends who had been his church treasurer for many years. John discovered a couple of days before he came to the conference that his friend had embezzled more than a million dollars from his church. He was really hurting, feeling betrayed and disillusioned. He began to pour out his heart to me.

John concluded his story with the statement, "I will never trust anyone like that again. I am going to put safeguards and double-checks into our church structure that require a high degree of accountability. I will never let someone do this to me again."

I knew he was speaking out of a lot of hurt, but I felt I needed to help him process his pain. I said to him, "John, the Bible says that Judas was a thief and Jesus knew it [see John 12:4-7]. Yet Jesus made Judas the treasurer of his ministry. Why would Jesus make Judas the treasurer when He knew that he was a thief?"

"I don't have any idea," he responded, as if it was a trick question.

"Well," I said, "there are only two reasons I can think of. The first one is that Jesus was trying to make Judas fail. But that doesn't seem like the Jesus I know."

John nodded in agreement.

"The second reason I can think of is that Jesus developed a culture of faith around Him. This faith culture was manifested in Jesus' trusting people before they deserved it. This resulted in eleven men becoming world-changers and one man hanging himself."

"World-changers are only developed in a culture of faith. Faith requires risk, and the nature of risk is that sometimes you lose," I continued. "John, it is probably wise for you to put more checks and balances in your accounting system, but if you stop believing in your people you won't create world-changers!" I went on to explain that while I believe in people around me, it is the people who have believed in me who have actually changed me the most. My friend was stunned and relieved.

If you don't produce a Judas now and then, you don't trust people as much as you should and you are reducing the number of Peters you will produce. The Kingdom is entered into by faith, lived in through faith, and extended with faith manifested through risk!

Risk opens the door to the *great adventure* in God. This reminds me of the years we lived in the Trinity Alps. We, like most others, had a four-wheel-drive vehicle because we needed it in the winter to get around. We were pretty broke, so we would go four-wheeling for entertainment. We would put our Jeep in two-wheel drive and venture through the mountains until we got stuck. Then we would put it in four-wheel drive to get out. Later on we bought a winch so that we could travel in four-wheel drive until we bogged down and then winch ourselves out. If you have never been stuck before, there is a bunch of gorgeous country you have never seen!

The supernatural nature of the Kingdom lies off-road. You can't get there in your Lexus, Cadillac, or Lincoln. If comfort, safety, and dignity are your gods, you will be confined to the pavement of religion and never discover the true beauty of His amazing world that lies just on the other side of the fear of man. There's a reason that the One sent to guide you into the realms of the Spirit is called the Comforter. If you follow Him, you're going to need one.

CHAPTER 4

Wearing Son-Glasses

～

Jesus called His 12 leaders *apostles*. Jesus borrowed the word *apostle* from the Romans who ruled the Jews of His day. Apostles were Roman generals who were specifically charged with reforming the culture of the nations they conquered. They taught the conquered people the Roman ways, rules, and customs. The Romans understood that unless they were able to implement Roman culture in these places, they would not be able to sustain a ruling relationship over them. In the same way, an apostolic culture is required for the reality of God's Kingdom to be sustained among a group of God's people. Much like the Roman generals of His day, Jesus sent His apostles out not only to heal the sick, get people saved, and proclaim the gospel, but also to establish a Kingdom culture among those who experienced these miracles.

Jesus' use of the term "apostle" indicates the power of culture either to sustain or restrain movements. This is something that I and the other leaders at Bethel Church have seen firsthand. Many leaders come to Bethel or other similar churches and see people moving in power, then try to replicate it at their own churches back home. They teach their people how to walk in miracles, heal the sick, and prophesy, but they don't understand that their culture won't sustain a real move of God. Soon their people return to a powerless lifestyle.

There is a big difference between ministering in the gifts of the Spirit and developing a supernatural culture inside of us that ultimately allows the Kingdom to flow through us. The contrast between supernatural ministry and a supernatural culture reminds me of the difference between air-conditioned automobiles sold in the early 1960s and cars sold today. If you bought a car with air conditioning in the early '60s, everybody knew you had it. The huge monstrosity of an air conditioning unit hung from the bottom of your dashboard. Like a pimple on the end of your nose, you couldn't miss it. The dealer installed all the early air conditioning units because the manufacturers had yet to begin installing them at the factory. Because these cars were not designed with air conditioning in mind, there were some major sacrifices a person had to make to stay cool. For instance, if you turned the unit on while the car was idling, it would stall. If you were going up a mountain with the air on, the vehicle would overheat; and if you decided for some silly reason that you needed to pass someone on a hot summer day, you had to turn the thing off so you would have the power to pass.

Of course, none of this is true of air conditioning in the automobiles of today. Vehicles are now conceived and designed with air conditioning in mind. The mechanical engineer knows the car is going to have air conditioning, so he integrates all the ductwork into the interior of the vehicle in a way that makes it one with the decor. The electrical engineer designs the wiring harnesses with all the looms set up for the air conditioning system. The architect of the cooling system develops the entire system knowing there will be air conditioning in the vehicle, and the list goes on and on. Everybody who designs these vehicles does so with air conditioning in mind.

Now when the driver wants air conditioning, he simply pushes a button on the dash. The switch doesn't actually turn the air compressor on, but it sends a message to the computer informing it that the driver wants it cooler. Next, the computer sends a message to the cooling fans demanding they come on and that the engine management system produce more horsepower so the A/C compressor can be turned on. Finally, the alternator is instructed to raise the electrical output to meet the increased load on the system. This all leads to a cool driver who is completely unaware of the intricacies of air conditioning, because it was all developed with the end in mind.

When people who don't have the core values of the Kingdom built into their thinking and lifestyle try to operate in supernatural ministry, they experience problems similar to an air-conditioned car from the '60s. Every time this kind of supernatural ministry is functioning, the Church stalls, overheats, or loses momentum. I can't count the number of times I have talked to church leaders who want nothing to do with prophecy, healing, deliverance, or miracles because the ministry they were exposed to was destructive instead of constructive. The gifts of the Spirit are the love language of God.

On the other hand, like the modern automobiles of today, when the power ministry is integrated fully into a culture built upon core values of the Kingdom, people experience the passion of Jesus every time they have a power encounter. After all, the gifts of the Spirit are the love language of God. When people experience a healing, they should feel loved by the Father. Prophecy should be the embrace of God Himself. And folks shouldn't need to be delivered from their last deliverance. We should never demonstrate the power of God at the expense of the character and nature of Jesus.

The gifts of the Spirit are the love language of God.

BEING DEAD RIGHT

I have heard many people describe a harsh believer in their church as a prophet, or a joyless Christian as an intercessor. Since when are *rude, depressed,* and *somber* fruits of the Spirit? Where do people get the idea that the Holy Spirit leaves His nature behind when He demonstrates His power? We never have permission to move in power in a way that misrepresents the love of God.

I remember watching a Christian television show several years ago that reminds me of what happens when someone speaks for the King, but leaves the core values of the Kingdom behind. In describing this man's mistake, please know that I do have a lot of respect for him. I have made many mistakes in the ministry myself.

This great prophet called a woman to the front of a packed auditorium on live TV. He began describing what he was seeing in his spirit with great accuracy, and in a dramatic fashion.

He prophesied, "I see your husband. He is coming home on such and such a street. But wait, he is turning...yes he is turning and going down another street. Oh, where is he going? He is going to another woman's house...Now I see your teenage son. He has a poster over his bed of a certain rock band. But what is it I see in the upper right-hand drawer of his dresser? Look in the upper right-hand drawer of his dresser. And I see your father. Yes, he is coming into your room... Oh, what is he doing? Oh, he is molesting you! He is molesting you!"

"No," she yelled, "that's not true!"

"Yes!" he insisted. "Yes, it is true!"

She fell down on the floor screaming and crying, humiliated in front of thousands of people, both in the audience and those watching the show at home. What did she do to deserve having her reputation smashed to bits? How would this woman ever face her family again? How would her son feel about his sin exposed on live television in the name of God? Where was the love in all of this? What happened to honor and respect? There is such a thing as being *dead* right!

Many people think if they got the word of knowledge or prophecy *right*, then their ministry was justified. Remember the Tree of the Knowledge of Good and Evil in the Garden of Eden? The Tree of the Knowledge of Good and Evil didn't give Adam and Eve life. It was only the fruit from the Tree of Life that released eternity into the souls of men. Getting words of knowledge right, like the Tree of Knowledge in the Garden of Eden, doesn't necessarily give life to the person on the receiving end of your ministry. There is such a thing as being DEAD right!

The story of Noah and his three sons demonstrates how exposing someone's sins to others can lead to death:

> *Then Noah began farming and planted a vineyard. He drank of the wine and became drunk, and uncovered himself inside his tent. Ham, the father of Canaan, saw the nakedness of his father, and told his two brothers outside. But Shem and Japheth took a garment and laid it upon both their shoulders and walked backward and covered the nakedness of their father; and their faces were turned away, so that they did not see their father's nakedness. When Noah awoke from his wine, he knew what his youngest son had done to him. So he said, "Cursed be Canaan; a servant of servants he shall be to his brothers." He also said, "Blessed be the Lord, the God of Shem; and let Canaan be his servant. May God enlarge Japheth, and let him dwell in the tents of Shem; and let Canaan be his servant"* (Genesis 9:20-27).

There is such a thing as being dead right!

Ham exposed his father's sin to his brothers. He didn't lie about his father's failure, but his actions resulted in a curse on his own life. The curse on Ham's life cost him his legacy. Hundreds of years later, Joshua drove the Canaanites out of their own land because of the curse that was on their great-grandfather Ham!

I should make it clear that oftentimes when people are stuck in sin, they need to be confronted in a redemptive way. However, if we abandon the core values of love, honor, and respect, we can be right about their issues, but we will most likely fail to help them come to true repentance. Again, remember that it is the kindness of God that leads to repentance (see Rom. 2:4). Love is a higher core value in the Kingdom than being right, and if you get that backwards, you won't release the reality of the Kingdom in your ministry. The core values of the Kingdom and the fruit of the Spirit are the walls of salvation, ensuring that our ministry is actually expanding the Kingdom and not killing people.

DISCIPLESHIP

We have to be careful not to try to do with prophecy, or any of the gifts of the Spirit for that matter, what God meant for us to accomplish through discipleship. Discipleship is the process of developing people through teaching, training, discipline, correction, and encouragement. Sometimes, in the vacuum of true discipleship, we try to compensate by correcting people with prophecy when they really need someone to come alongside them and disciple them.

I learned this many years ago through some words I heard a prophet give. He was a really good man but he struggled in his ability to father his own children. Several times a year he would stand up in church and give corrective prophetic words to his teenagers. He was a strong prophet but an inexperienced father, so he tried to make up for his weak fathering with his strong prophetic gift. Of course, his children would leave church embarrassed and humiliated.

Similarly, Christ commissioned the Church to disciple nations, which means to assume a role of training and fathering (see Matt. 28). I wonder how much of the negative prophecy that is being proclaimed over the nations is really the result of the Body of Christ not understanding how to father the nations.

DELIVERANCE

Deliverance is another one of the power gifts that needs to embody the loving hands of God and the core values of the Kingdom. I have heard from countless people whose stories of deliverance sound like something out of the Twilight Zone. One lady told me that her pastor pours salt on the oppressed to get them free (a crazy but true story)! We can and should cast out demons without dishonoring the people they are holding captive. Let me illustrate this.

> *Demons respond only to authority.*

Some time ago I was speaking at a conference in a wonderful church in Nevada. As I closed my message, I shared a little bit of my testimony of how the Lord had freed me from demonic oppression as a young Christian. When I exited the platform, several pastors escorted me to the green room for a break before the next session. On the way, a young, beautiful woman approached me and asked to talk to me. My escorts tried to direct her to the team of people who were there to pray for the needy, but she persisted to try to talk to me. I finally stopped and motioned for her to come over.

By now we were in the hallway with many leaders surrounding us. As she approached, I could see she was very tormented. She put her head on my shoulder and began weeping uncontrollably. I leaned over towards her, and she whispered in my ear that her father repeatedly molested her all the years she was growing up, leaving her broken, ashamed, and extremely oppressed. As I started to pray for her deliverance, she suddenly fell to the floor in a seizure-like demonic manifestation. She was screaming and writhing on the carpet as several leaders looked on. I got down on the floor and put my arm around her to steady her head and embrace her. I started talking softly in her ear, telling her that she was going to be okay.

"Jesus loves you and He is here to help you," I said.

Then I began to lead her in prayers of forgiveness for several people who had abused her. The entire time I was simply whispering in her ear and having her quietly forgive them. When she had finished forgiving everyone that the Holy Spirit showed her she was bitter with, I calmly and quietly commanded the evil spirits to leave her. A few minutes later she rose to her feet crying and laughing for joy. She was a free, happy young woman!

When we arrived at the green room, the leaders were buzzing with questions. The first one asked, "What happened out there?"

"A young lady got delivered," I responded.

Another asked, "How come you didn't raise your voice when you made the demons leave?"

"Demons don't respond to volume; they respond to authority. The demons are the ones that have the loud voices when they come out, not the minister," I answered.

We talked for more than an hour about not losing the heart of the King when we move in the power of His Kingdom. So many times the dignity of a person is lost at the expense of their deliverance, but it doesn't need to be that way. Demons respond only to authority.

CORE VALUES DEFINED

I have been talking a lot about developing ministry inside the core values of the Kingdom, but what are core values and how do they affect our ministry? I am glad you asked. Core values are the principles, standards, and virtues at the center of the way we live, love, and think. Our core values are the prophets of our destiny. They dictate what we allow ourselves to desire and they decide what is critical to accomplish in our lives. Core values are at the center of the way we live, love, and think.

> *Core values are at the center of the way we live, love, and think.*
>
> ෴

Our core values give us answers years before we even know what the questions are. They make choices for us long before we know what the outcome will ever be. For example: A 13-year-old young woman decides that she is going to be a virgin until she marries. When she is older she finally meets the man of her dreams, but he wants to take her to bed. She doesn't have to wrestle over what to do, because the core values she embraced many years ago have limited her options. She doesn't know how her decision will affect her relationship with Romeo, but she decided who she would *be* long before she decided who she would be with.

It is important to understand that core values are different from high values. Our core values set the boundaries for our behavior. They tell us how to act in our ministry, friendships, family relationships, business dealings, and conflicts. They are the referees in our relationships. I will sacrifice for my high values but I would die for my core values. For instance, I have a car equipped with air conditioning. I paid a couple thousand dollars more to have a cool car, and it costs me gas mileage every time I use it. I have a high value for comfort. I will sacrifice to be cool but I won't die for it. Core values are different from high values because they aren't just something I do; they are the fiber of my being, the very essence of who I am.

DISCOVERING YOUR CORE VALUES

I began intentionally discovering and developing my core values, the things that I will live and die for, a few years ago. I use the word "discover" because everybody has core values, even if they aren't the core values of the Kingdom. As I found out in my own life, three things are likely to happen if you ask people to make a list of their core values.

1. They will make a list of high values they don't really live by, but know they should.

2. They will be completely unaware of the real core values that dictate most of their decisions, as most of our deepest convictions often lie below the conscious level.

3. They will discover that many of the decisions they make often come from the wrong core values.

In 2002, I was staying on a small island in the South Pacific for a week, getting alone with God, and working through some heart issues in my own life. The Lord began to deal with me about renewing my mind to live from Kingdom virtues that would guide my decisions the rest of my life. He showed me that living by His virtues would simplify my life, as they would become my life coach. Here are the virtues He gave me:

THE VIRTUES I LIVE BY

✧ I will serve God first and honor Him always, both in life and in death.

✧ I will be honest, loyal, trustworthy, and a man of my word, no matter what the price.

✧ I will keep my values, no matter how much they cost me, and if I fail, I will be quick to repent.

✧ I will treat all people with respect and honor, whether they are friend or foe, as they were created in God's image.

✧ I will strive to love everyone despite their opinions, attitudes, or persuasions, no matter how they treat me.

✧ **I will never act out of fear, fear any man or demon, or make decisions strictly to save my life. I will fear God only.**

- ✧ I will be loyal to my wife both in thought and deed into eternity.

- ✧ I will live to bless and empower the generations to come and leave a legacy, both in the Spirit and in the natural, to a people yet to be born.

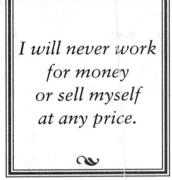

> *I will never work for money or sell myself at any price.*

- ✧ I will never work for money or sell myself at any price. I will only be motivated to do what I believe to be right and receive my substance from God. I vow to be generous under all circumstances.

- ✧ I will live my life to bring out the best in people and bring them into an encounter with the real and living God.

- ✧ I will live my life in the supernatural realm, expecting and anticipating God to do the impossible to me, through me, and around me as I follow Him.

- ✧ It is my lifetime ambition to become friends with God in the deepest sense of the word.

- ✧ I dedicate my strength, my wealth, all that I am, and all that I will ever be to see the course of world history altered until the kingdom of this world becomes the Kingdom of our God.

- ✧ I will never work for money or sell myself at any price.

Our virtues and life in God were really put to the test when Kathy and I came to Bethel Church in 1998. We had two businesses and several employees when Bill Johnson asked us to join the Bethel team and begin the School of Supernatural Ministry. One of the greatest challenges was that Bethel couldn't pay us a salary for nine months. We had to leave the home we built 17 years before, the place we raised our children, to come to Redding and live in an apartment. But we had decided a long time ago that our souls were not for sale and we would never work for money. We would only live for God and trust Him completely to take care of our needs and our desires. Our core values simplified our decision because all we needed to know was whether God was in this move or not. The answer is history.

> *We often question what we hear but not how we hear.*
>
> ✿

CORE VALUES ARE THE LENSES OF LIFE

As you can see, core values are the virtues we live by, but they are more than that. They are also the lenses through which we view life. Jesus made a powerful statement in Luke's Gospel that helps to clarify this point. He said, *"...so take care **how** you listen..."* (Luke 8:18). We will often question what we hear, but seldom question *how* we hear. This principle also applies to seeing. Many times we question what we see but we hardly ever question *how* we see. We often question what we hear but not *how* we hear. Core values are the lenses that lie over our hearts, interpreting the events of our world. Jesus explained it this way:

> *The eye is the lamp of the body; so then if your eye is clear, your whole body will be full of light. But if your eye is bad, your whole body will be full of darkness. If then the light that is in you is darkness, how great is the darkness!* (Matthew 6:22-23)

When we have pain or brokenness in our hearts, it is like we're wearing dark lenses over our souls. We begin to view the world not as it is, but as we are. The darkness in our own souls reinterprets life, creating a perverted reality. Here is an example that might help you connect to what I am saying. We view the world not as it is, but as we are.

Bill Johnson and I did a crusade in Mexico in 2004 that was attended by a couple thousand people. Bill preached the first two sessions, and I preached the last session. We were seeing great fruit and a bunch of miracles. I was very excited to have the last night so that I could bring the crusade to the ultimate climax. But my Mexican interpreter had other ideas. My theme was, "Christ will change you from a sinner to a saint." The struggle was that my interpreter was raised in a denomination that only made famous *dead* people saints. So he reinterpreted my message to agree with his belief system. I don't know a word of Spanish, so I was clueless about what was happening. But I did notice the same people who were very responsive when Bill preached seemed cold, stale, and dead when I spoke. I got down off the stage and my mind was spinning. What happened? I couldn't figure it out. Just as I exited the stage, several of the bilingual Mexican pastors rushed over to me and explained the situation.

Core values are like my Mexican interpreter. If they are clean, pure, and right, you hear what was really being said through life and perceive what is real. But, if your interpreter has a prejudice, what you see and believe to be real will be a perversion of the truth.

Our minds have the amazing ability to process an incredible amount of external stimuli and use it to interpret reality. For instance, scientists have discovered that the optic nerve is designed in a way that causes us to see everything upside down. But our brains receive other information from the rest of our body, and make a decision to reinterpret our reality by reversing the image to create what our minds believe to be real. This process is amazing, unless our brains *misinterpret* the facts in a way that leads us to *misbehave*. Let me illustrate this.

Years ago I went to school to get my pilot's license. I never did finish, but I did complete the ground school. Our instructors beat it into our heads not to trust our mind's perceptions when we

We view the world not as it is, but as we are.

75

were flying in clouds, but instead to believe our instruments. There is something called *spatial disorientation* that often causes pilots, in severe weather, to feel like their plane is upside down and rising when in fact it is actually the opposite. The pilot turns the plane upside down and points it towards the ground, thinking he is leveling it out. This usually results in the plane crashing right into the ground! When this happens, it is because the pilot experienced a virtual reality—it looked real, felt real, and seemed logical, but it wasn't real.

Our core values are the instruments of our soul that keep us flying upright through the storms of life. Each Kingdom core value is like a different gauge directing us in the affairs of our life and ministry. When we lose touch with the heart of the King—and true core values are the heart of the King—we end up colliding with the ground. Those who are flying with us, as well as those who are innocently grounded, become casualties of our ministry. Our core values keep us flying upright through the storms.

VIEWING THE WORLD THROUGH A LOGJAM

Jesus said:

> *Why do you look at the speck that is in your brother's eye, but do not notice the log that is in your own eye? Or how can you say to your brother, "Let me take the speck out of your eye," and behold, the log is in your own eye? You hypocrite, first take the log out of your own eye, and then you will see clearly to take the speck out of your brother's eye* (Matthew 7:3-5).

Our core values keep us flying upright through the storms.

This is a picture of what happens when we try to minister to others with a skewed set of core values. If our core values are not based on the truth, we will consistently misdiagnose the problems of the world around us, and thus fail to treat them in an appropriate way. We simply cannot help people with our supernatural ministry when we are viewing the world through a worthless value system (a "log" made of wood, hay, or stubble), which blinds us to the King's perspective. It is no wonder that so many believers can't find anything beautiful in the world or refuse to see the treasure lying in the lives of sinners. They are looking through a logjam!

> *The key to building a Kingdom worldview is heavenly revelation of eternal reality.*
> ∽

Most of the time our opinions of others are more of a commentary on who we are than on who others are. For example, if I don't feel good about my performance at work, I will begin to build a case against my coworkers who are high performers. My opinion of them is affected by my own disappointment in myself. I view them through the lens of jealousy and my assessment of them is really a commentary on my own heart and life.

Poor people often view the rich like this. Because someone has something that they can't seem to attain, they build a case against them: "They are tax evaders. They should be punished for having money. Money is evil and these people are selfish; or they oppressed, stepped on, or used people to get rich." This could be true in some cases, but *to have this opinion of someone without knowing them personally* is a sign that you are a "log-jamitist"! This is a serious condition of the heart where your foot gets stuck in your face.

It is important that the eyes of our heart are clear so we view the world through our special "Son-glasses." Paul put it this way:

> *I pray that the eyes of your heart may be enlightened, so that you will know what is the hope of His calling, what are the riches of the glory of His inheritance in the saints, and what is the surpassing greatness of His power toward*

us who believe. These are in accordance with the working of the strength of His might which He brought about in Christ, when He raised Him from the dead and seated Him at His right hand in the heavenly places, far above all rule and authority and power and dominion, and every name that is named, not only in this age but also in the one to come (Ephesians 1:18-21).

The word "enlighten" in this passage is the Greek word *photizo*, which is where we get our word "photosynthesis," meaning, "to build with light." Paul says that the key to building a Kingdom worldview is *heavenly revelation of eternal reality.* This revelation creates the foundation for our worldview from three primary things—the hope of His calling, the glorious riches of His inheritance in the saints, and His power for those who believe. All these realities have been made available to us through Christ. This revelation of Christ will alter our reality so we are guided by the core values of the Kingdom as we interpret and negotiate our way through the circumstances of life. We certainly can't represent Jesus and continue His supernatural ministry unless our hearts have been enlightened by the revelation of who He really is, what He has done, and what He is doing. The key to building a Kingdom worldview is heavenly revelation of eternal reality.

Our core values affect the way we view God, the devil, ourselves, and the world, and therefore they have a huge impact on the way we minister. They interpret the way events in life relate to God and which circumstances in life we attribute to God. For example, if we believe that God is angry, we will interpret world events through this lens. We will view natural disasters, terrorist attacks, and famines as acts of God (I talk about this in greater detail in the "Graceland" chapter). Who God is *to us*, He will be *through us*! It is so important that we have a pure heart, because it is only the pure in heart (those who have clear lenses) that see God. An angry God creates harsh, judgmental, and graceless ministers. Who God is *to us*, He will be *through us*!

FINDING YOUR PLACE IN CHRIST

Paul taught us that Christ's Body is made up of many members that have different functions:

> *Who God is to us, He will be through us!*

For even as the body is one and yet has many members, and all the members of the body, though they are many, are one body, so also is Christ. For by one Spirit we were all baptized into one body, whether Jews or Greeks, whether slaves or free, and we were all made to drink of one Spirit. For the body is not one member, but many. If the foot says, "Because I am not a hand, I am not a part of the body," it is not for this reason any the less a part of the body. And if the ear says, "Because I am not an eye, I am not a part of the body," it is not for this reason any the less a part of the body. If the whole body were an eye, where would the hearing be? If the whole were hearing, where would the sense of smell be? But now God has placed the members, each one of them, in the body, just as He desired. If they were all one member, where would the body be? But now there are many members, but one body. And the eye cannot say to the hand, "I have no need of you"; or again the head to the feet, "I have no need of you" (1 Corinthians 12:12-21).

How do you figure out what part of the Body of Christ you are? Someone once said, "You are not what you think you are and you are not what others think you are. But often you become what you *think* others think you are." In other words, we become the reflection of our perception of others' thoughts towards us. John Maxwell said, "Most of us become what the most important person in our life thinks we should become." This principle really

> *"Most of us become what the most important person in our life thinks we should become."*
>
> ❧

works in our favor when the most important person in our life is God and the lens of our life is clear. If we are becoming what we think God thinks of us, and our perception of God's thoughts towards us are accurate, then we really are being transformed into the image of God! "Most of us become what the most important person in our life thinks we should become."

When the lens that lies over our heart is clean and clear, we will know what our place in the Body is by the way in which we view God Himself. Again, who God is to us, He will be through us. The story in Matthew's Gospel is a great example of this:

Now when Jesus came into the district of Caesarea Philippi, He was asking His disciples, "Who do people say that the Son of Man is?" And they said, "Some say John the Baptist; and others, Elijah; but still others, Jeremiah, or one of the prophets." He said to them, "But who do you say that I am?" Simon Peter answered, "You are the Christ, the Son of the living God." And Jesus said to him, "Blessed are you, Simon Barjona, because flesh and blood did not reveal this to you, but My Father who is in heaven. I also say to you that you are Peter, and upon this rock I will build My church; and the gates of Hades will not overpower it. I will give you the keys of the kingdom of heaven; and whatever you bind on earth shall have been bound in heaven, and whatever you loose on earth shall have been loosed in heaven" (Matthew 16:13-19).

Jesus asked a question, "Who do you say that I am?" Another way to say it is, "Who am I to you?" Peter got this revelation: "You are the Christ, the Son of the living God." We know that Jesus is not just the Christ; He is also the Bread of Life, the Lamb of God, the Great Shepherd and so on. But Peter saw Him as the Christ. *Christ* means the "anointed one" or "the anointed Messiah." Jesus responded to Peter's statement with another revelation: "The gates of Hades will not overpower the Church and you (Peter) will receive keys of authority to bind and loose." Can you see that Peter's revelation of Jesus was connected to the revelation of his own calling? He saw Jesus as the powerful Christ and then he was told that he also had authority and power.

Significantly, the revelation of Peter's destiny came with a name change. *Simon Barjona* became *Peter*, meaning "a piece of rock," because he was the one who received the revelation that Christ is the *rock* upon which the Church is built! It's almost like it takes one to know one. Christ essentially told Peter, "I'm the Rock, and you're a chip off this old block." I may be belaboring the point here, but I am trying to help you understand that "if your eye is clear" (you have the Kingdom's core values), then your view of God actually helps you know what your life's calling is and what part you play in the Body of Christ. You don't see God the way He is (in His fullness) but you tend to see God the way you are.

In other words, when you describe God to someone, you are really describing yourself, the person who God is supposed to be through you.

CORE VALUES FOR SUPERNATURAL MINISTRY

The leadership at Bethel Church began proactively developing our core values for our supernatural ministry years ago. It is not so important that you adopt the same core values, but that you seek the Lord for the values that represent the part of the King's Body that you are to portray. I will list a few of ours here for the sake of example.

- ✧ God wants to speak to us more than we want to listen. After all, how can a Person named "The Word of God" not want to talk to people? This core value creates an expectation in our hearts to hear Him at any moment.

✧ All things work in our favor when we serve God, no matter what the circumstances look like. This core value trains us to look for and focus on God's redemptive purposes more than problems. *"We know that God causes all things to work together for good to those who love God, to those who are called according to His purpose"* (Rom. 8:28).

✧ God loved us before we loved Him, and He never stops loving us. We never have to earn His love through good works. This core value trains us to focus on His love more than our lack, and to trust that we have an unlimited source of love to give every person we meet. *"We love, because He first loved us"* (1 John 4:19).

✧ Fear is not a part of God's love and therefore it shouldn't be a part of our supernatural ministry. This trains us to respond rather than react to any kind of intimidation of the enemy. *"There is no fear in love; but perfect love casts out fear, because fear involves punishment, and the one who fears is not perfected in love"* (1 John 4:18).

✧ God has plans for our welfare and blessing. He has no plans for calamity in our life. This trains us to see difficulty as an opportunity for God to bless us and bring us more fully into His purposes for our lives. It also creates an expectation for God to bless us richly so we can be a blessing to others. It prevents us from coming under a poverty mind-set. *"'For I know the plans that I have for you,' declares the Lord, 'plans for welfare and not for calamity to give you a future and a hope'"* (Jer. 29:11).

✧ We are a special, holy, and royal people. This core value trains us to value others and ourselves as the precious possessions of God, for whom He sacrificed His only Son. It fosters a culture of honor in which we treat others as royalty because we are royalty. *"But you are a **chosen race**, a **royal priesthood**, a **holy nation**, a people for God's own **possession**, so that you may proclaim the excellencies of*

Him who has called you out of darkness into His marvelous light" (1 Pet. 2:9).

✧ We are to overcome and overpower anything evil that is against us. This core value prevents us from thinking of ourselves as victims of circumstance and frees us to think from a perspective in which nothing is impossible. It enables us to look for creative and extravagant solutions to problems. *"But in all these things we overwhelmingly conquer through Him who loved us"* (Rom. 8:37).

✧ The devil is evil and is behind all the bad stuff in the world. Jesus is always good and does all the great things. We are called to destroy the works of the devil with our supernatural ministry. This core value keeps the lines of battle clearly drawn so that we are not directing *judgment* at people, but instead are bringing them the justice that Jesus purchased for them on the cross. *"The Son of God appeared for this purpose, to destroy the works of the devil"* (1 John 3:8b). *"The thief comes only to steal and kill and destroy; I came that they may have life, and have it abundantly"* (John 10:10).

✧ We were born to rule through the power of the Kingdom and the love of God. This core value enables us to perceive the authorities and kingdoms of the world from an eternal perspective, so that our faith and intercession are founded firmly on the dominion of Christ. *"Then the sovereignty, the dominion and the greatness of all the kingdoms under the whole heaven will be given to the people of the saints of the Highest One; His kingdom will be an everlasting kingdom, and all the dominions will serve and obey Him"* (Dan. 7:27).

✧ We are God's friends and He tells us His secrets. This core value reminds us that God wants us to live in intimacy with Him far above obedience. He is calling us to move beyond slavery and co-reign with Christ. *"No longer do I call you slaves, for the slave does not know what his master is doing; but I have called you friends, for all things that I have heard from My Father I have made known to you"* (John 15:15).

✧ Signs and wonders follow all **believers**, not just a few special people. This core value trains every member of the Body of Christ to think of themselves as carriers of the power of God who are available for miraculous assignments. *"These signs will accompany those who have believed: in My name they will cast out demons, they will speak with new tongues; they will pick up serpents, and if they drink any deadly poison, it will not hurt them; they will lay hands on the sick, and they will recover"* (Mark 16:17-18).

✧ We have inherited the divine nature and grow in the fruit of the Spirit as we hang out with God. This core value trains us to embrace the journey of maturity as a process of yielding to the work of God within us and keeps us from a striving mentality. *"But the fruit of the Spirit is love, joy, peace, patience, kindness, goodness, faithfulness, gentleness, self-control; against such things there is no law"* (Gal. 5:22-23). *"For by these He has granted to us His precious and magnificent promises, so that by them you may become partakers of the divine nature, having escaped the corruption that is in the world by lust"* (2 Pet. 1:4).

Again, these are a few of the core values that we desire to carry into our supernatural ministry so that the power of the King and love of the Kingdom flow together. I urge you to discover and develop your core values so that your life and ministry can be firmly founded on Christ's perspective.

CHAPTER 5

Living in Graceland

The world is full of walking wounded—those whose hearts have met the bloody end of the sword of judgment. Often wielding the sword are people who call themselves Christians but act more like self-commissioned Old Testament prophets who believe their job is to judge the hearts of men and punish the wickedness of the planet. These wild-eyed wonders spend their lives looking for a fight with sinners, but the real conflict is with the sinner inside them. Though they may know that Jesus died for their sins, they still live with troubled souls that long for mercy but expect judgment. Oh, that these sons of God would be enlightened by the gospel they claim to know! The world is full of walking wounded.

The full revelation of what the Cross accomplished in history is so dynamic that those who experience it are literally translated from the province of bondage to the gates of "Graceland." Leaving the old country of death and despair behind, these folks come into the new world of mercy and hope. The people who successfully leave the old paradigm and begin to live in this new reality are those who understand that there is a dramatic difference between the ministry of the Old Covenant and the supernatural ministry of the New Covenant. While the ministry of both covenants is marked by divine demonstrations of power, the driving purpose behind these displays is completely different.

Christians who come to the shores of this new world called the Kingdom but persist in walking in judgment, have brought the stone tablets of the old country with them. These folks have a B.C. mind-set—they understand the fact that sin requires judgment, but fail to realize that the wrath of God poured out on the Cross of Christ quenched the fires of judgment, unlocking the treasure of mercy in the heart of God Himself. People who don't believe that the blood of Jesus altered Heaven's perspective towards this planet scare me! They create a schizophrenic culture because they bring the cold steel values of the Old Covenant into their grace-filled life in Christ. This usually results in a strange mixture of judgment and mercy that is not only confusing but is also self-mutilating, faultfinding, and often downright heartless. The Cross of Christ quenched the fires of judgment—unlocking the heart of God.

The world is full of walking wounded.

It seems to me that the Body of Christ is in need of some teaching that exposes the divided thinking behind these conflicting attitudes. At the foundation of this thinking is a misunderstanding of the nature of the Old and New Covenants. The Old and New Covenants are essentially two different relationships between mankind and God. These relationships are mutually exclusive because the conditions under which these covenants were made were entirely opposite. Let's explore these two relationships by starting with life under the Old Covenant.

HATE WHAT I HATE…

In the Old Testament, a believer's zeal for God was measured by his hatred for those who didn't walk with the Lord. This attitude was cultivated by Jehovah Himself! From Genesis to Malachi, God, in the name of justice and righteousness, was personally responsible for the killing of millions of sinners. Much like the Muslim suicide bombers who blow themselves up for the sake of their god, zealous Old Testament saints destroyed unbelievers in the name of Jehovah and were commended for it by God Himself. A believer's zeal for God was measured by his hatred for unbelievers.

> *The Cross of Christ quenched the fires of judgment—unlocking the heart of God.*

Jesus contrasted the Old and New Testament attitude of God when He taught:

> *You have heard that it was said, "You shall love your neighbor and hate your enemy." But I say to you, love your enemies and pray for those who persecute you, so that you may be sons of your Father who is in heaven; for He causes His sun to rise on the evil and the good, and sends rain on the righteous and the unrighteous* (Matthew 5:43-45).

Jesus said, "You have heard it said." Where do you think they heard "hate your enemies" from? Well, I'll tell you, they got it from the Old Testament writers, because that was the attitude of our God under the Old Covenant. Here are a few Old Testament Scriptures that make this crystal clear.

> *No Ammonite or Moabite shall enter the assembly of the Lord; none of their descendants, even to the tenth generation, shall ever enter the assembly of the Lord, because they did not meet you with food and water on the way when you*

came out of Egypt, and because they hired against you Balaam the son of Beor from Pethor of Mesopotamia, to curse you. Nevertheless, the Lord your God was not willing to listen to Balaam, but the Lord your God turned the curse into a blessing for you because the Lord your God loves you. You shall never seek their peace or their prosperity all your days (Deuteronomy 23:3-6).

So now do not give your daughters to their sons nor take their daughters to your sons, and never seek their peace or their prosperity, that you may be strong and eat the good things of the land and leave it as an inheritance to your sons forever (Ezra 9:12).

Jehu the son of Hanani the seer went out to meet him and said to King Jehoshaphat, "Should you help the wicked and love those who hate the Lord and so bring wrath on yourself from the Lord?" (2 Chronicles 19:2)

I hate the assembly of evildoers, and I will not sit with the wicked (Psalm 26:5).

I hate those who regard vain idols, but I trust in the Lord (Psalm 31:6).

The story of King Saul is a great illustration of the attitude of judgment that prevailed before the blood of Christ. Saul lost his throne because he showed mercy to an enemy king named Agag, despite the fact that God, through the prophet Samuel, had told him to kill him. When Samuel arrived on the scene, he rebuked King Saul for his unauthorized mercy, stripped the throne from him, and hewed King Agag into pieces (see 1 Sam. 15).

> *A believer's zeal for God was measured by his hatred for unbelievers.*

Another example of God sanctioning the killing of thousands is found in the Book of Joshua. Here the Israelites

90

were commanded by Jehovah to go into the land of Canaan, kill everyone, and take their property for themselves.

> *For it was of the Lord to harden their hearts, to meet Israel in battle in order that he might utterly destroy them, that they might receive no mercy, but that he might destroy them, just as the Lord had commanded Moses* (Joshua 11:20).

Can you imagine going to church and having someone tell you that Jesus told him to kill everyone who had an abortion or committed adultery? You would be on the phone with the police department in five seconds! But these are the kinds of words that people in the Old Testament often heard from God.

GOD HAD TO DIE

Why is it that God was so tough on sinners under the Old Covenant? In order to answer this, we must understand the nature of a biblical covenant. A covenant is the deepest and most binding of relationships, and in ancient times it was an agreement enforced by death. For example, in that day if I were to buy a piece of land from someone and wanted to pay it off with monthly payments, I would make a covenant with the seller. We would gather some witnesses and verbalize our agreement in their presence. Next we would take a lamb or another animal, cut it in half, join hands, and walk through the two halves of the animal together. This meant our agreement was made over our dead bodies, or unto death. If one of us broke our agreement we would be killed. We see God make this type of covenant with Abraham in Genesis 15. God had to die so He could fulfill the requirements of the Law.

When God made a similar covenant with the people of Israel, it bound Him to His people unto death. God gave Israel the Law—the stipulations of the

God had to die so He could fulfill the requirements of the Law.

Old Covenant—with the full knowledge that their sinful state prevented them from fulfilling it. He did this to show them, and all of humanity, their need for Christ. God's black-and-white attitude towards sinners reveals the immensity of our debt and depravity so we can understand why we so desperately needed someone to help us. The Old Covenant's entire purpose was to set the stage for the New Covenant. But remember, a covenant is terminated only by death. Therefore God had to die so He could fulfill the requirements of the Law, create justice, and establish a new covenant, ultimately extending mercy to millions who don't deserve it.

GOD HAS ALWAYS WANTED RELATIONSHIP

The merciless nature of the Old Covenant wasn't a revelation of the heart of God as much as it was the concession He had to make in order to approach cold-hearted, sinful mankind and draw us back into relationship with Him. By the time God called Israel as His people, the cumulative effect of sin on the human race had so diminished their knowledge of God that He was unrecognizable to them as their Father and Creator. His overtures of relationship were perceived as threatening, so the people begged Him just to give them the rules and stay away. Moses, who had received the revelation of God's desire for friendship, was one of a handful in the Old Testament who discovered the heart of God for His people in making this covenant.

God's Heart:

> *Moses went up to God, and the Lord called to him from the mountain, saying, "Thus you shall say to the house of Jacob and tell the sons of Israel: 'You yourselves have seen what I did to the Egyptians, and how I bore you on eagles' wings, and brought you to Myself. Now then, if you will indeed obey My voice and keep My covenant, then you shall be My own possession among all the peoples, for all the earth is Mine; and you shall be to Me a kingdom of priests and a*

holy nation.' These are the words that you shall speak to the sons of Israel" (Exodus 19:3-6).

The people's response:

All the people perceived the thunder and the lightning flashes and the sound of the trumpet and the mountain smoking; and when the people saw it, they trembled and stood at a distance. Then they said to Moses, "Speak to us yourself and we will listen; but let not God speak to us, or we will die" (Exodus 20:18-19).

Sadly, this attitude was expressed over and over throughout the entire Old Testament. This ultimately led to an entire population trying to behave without knowing God. But righteousness has always been the fruit of humble people having a close, personal relationship with a holy God. When the people asked to live by rules instead of relationship, they chose to labor for their own righteousness, which was a setup for failure. Without relationship, God had to judge them according to their works instead of according to His. The choice they made to be justified by their own works led to an incredible debt that mounted against the entire human race. Mankind became a powerless prisoner of sin serving life sentences in the slave camp of satan. Without relationship, God judged according to man's works—not according to His.

How would God free the people He loved so much from their self-imposed bondage to the Law? How could He extend mercy to people who were guilty, without violating justice?

THE COURTROOM DRAMA

These questions make it clear that God had a challenge; He had to fulfill the debt of mankind so He could extend

> *Without relationship, God judged according to man's works—not according to His.*

mercy. This expresses the nature of His Kingdom—the foundation of His Supreme Court is built upon righteousness and justice, but His decrees are made from the Mercy Seat (see Ps. 89:14; Heb. 9:5).

Allow me to present some mock court case scenarios to demonstrate Heaven's predicament:

Let's say someone killed my wife and we went to court. While in court the judge says to the murderer, "Your father was a friend of mine. Yeah, we used to golf together every weekend. You're free to go." This would be mercy but it wouldn't be justice. (Have you ever seen a movie where the show ends with the bad guy being allowed to go free? It never sits well. Something in each of us needs justice.)

On the other hand, if the judge ordered the man's execution, this would be justice but it wouldn't be mercy.

Now, let's say the murderer's mother tries to intervene for her son, now on death row, by saying, "I will take my son's place. Please exchange my life for his." In Heaven's court, the Judge would look at his record of fugitives and find her name on the list. He would have to say, "You can't pay for your son's sins because we have a warrant out for your arrest for the sins you have committed!"

Remember, the Bible says, *"All have sinned and fall short of the glory of God"* (Rom. 3:23) and *"The wages of sin is death"* (Rom. 6:23). In other words, everyone owes their life for their own sin, so they can't offer their life to cover someone else's.

But then suddenly Jesus (the Judge's Son) steps into the courtroom and says, "Your Honor, I will give My life to redeem their lives!" The Judge looks for the record of the sins of Jesus and finds none, because He *never* sinned. The Judge decrees, "Yes, You can take his place. You don't owe for Your own sins, so You can offer Your life in exchange for his."

Now, if I were to say, "You can't let Jesus pay for that man's sins! He killed my wife!" the Judge would have to say, "Your wife was already on death row for her crimes. I am exchanging My sinless Son for your guilty wife."

Jesus' death on the Cross changed the conditions of mankind's standing before the Judge of Heaven. The judgment that provoked the wrath of God was poured out on Jesus when He died for the sins of the world. With justice fulfilled by His Son's blood, the Judge was free to extend mercy without being crooked.

Paul said it best: *"He made* [Jesus] *who knew no sin to be sin on our behalf, so that we might become the righteousness of God in Him"* (2 Cor. 5:21). In the Book of Romans Paul writes, *"*[Jesus] *was delivered over because of our transgressions, and was raised because of our justification"* (Rom. 4:25) and again he writes, *"...having now been justified by His blood, we shall be saved from the wrath of God through Him"* (Rom. 5:9).

Wow! When Jesus died for our sins, it enabled us to stand before God on the same ground as Jesus Himself. We have become the righteousness of God in Him, which means He can relate to us as sons and daughters instead of as sinners. And the covenant God makes with His children is completely different from the covenant He makes with sinners.

VIOLENT ACTS OF GRACE

Unlike the first covenant, which we were unable to fulfill through our own works, the second covenant expects us to act righteously because we have been made righteous in Christ. This is why Jesus made the statement we looked at earlier:

> *You have heard that it was said, "You shall love your neighbor and hate your enemy." **But** I say to you, love your enemies and pray for those who persecute you, so that you may be sons of your Father who is in heaven; for He causes His sun to rise on the evil and the good, and sends rain on the righteous and the unrighteous. For if you love those who love you, what reward do you have? Do not even the tax*

collectors do the same? If you greet only your brothers, what more are you doing than others? Do not even the Gentiles do the same? Therefore you are to be perfect, as your heavenly Father is perfect (Matthew 5:43-48).

At first glance it looks like the standard Jesus is raising is even more stringent than the original Law. Be perfect? But Jesus was showing us what God is really like—and what we can be like through His righteousness. God's perfection is most fully expressed in His ability to love everyone unconditionally, and this is what should characterize His people in the New Covenant. What an amazing contrast between this and the harsh Law of the Old Covenant.

Again, remember that for hundreds of years the Jews were told to have nothing to do with unbelievers, to detest, hate, and destroy them. When Jesus arrived on the scene with His "love evil men" doctrine, it was an incredible paradigm shift. Grace was beginning to invade their world of judgment.

Jesus went on to reinforce this dramatic contrast between the two covenants when He explained it further in the Book of Luke:

The Law and the Prophets were proclaimed until John; since that time the gospel of the kingdom of God has been preached, and everyone is forcing his way into it (Luke 16:16).

The Jews grew up reading the Law and the Prophets. The Law and the Prophets (the Old Testament/Covenant) said, "You can't come into the Kingdom because you are a sinner. Stay out, you rotten, no-good lawbreakers." But Jesus performed a violent act of grace by going to the Cross. The Cross became a battering ram that smashed the iron bars and bronze doors of judgment, forcing the unworthy (us) into the Kingdom of

> *The Cross smashed the iron bars and bronze doors of judgment.*

God (see Isa. 45:2). The Cross smashed the iron bars and bronze doors of judgment.

The reason they had to force their way into the Kingdom, however, was that there was opposition from the very people who should have recognized the paradigm shift Christ had come to bring. Instead, the scribes and Pharisees stood guard as gatekeepers of the Old Covenant's prison doors. Jesus rebuked them for trying to keep us out of the Kingdom:

> *But woe to you, scribes and Pharisees, hypocrites, because you shut off the kingdom of heaven from people; for you do not enter in yourselves, nor do you allow those who are entering to go in* (Matthew 23:13).

Sadly, there are still religious leaders today who work to block the entrance of Heaven by using the Law to disqualify the candidates of conversion. But hungry people still get desperate enough to force their way past the gatekeepers into the Kingdom.

THE WILL AND TESTAMENT

Jesus prepared His disciples to understand what His death would accomplish at the Last Supper. This dinner would go down as the most significant meal in history. It was Passover, the day the Jews celebrated escaping the judgment of God in Egypt during the time of Moses. God's judgment passed over them because they had the blood of a lamb sprinkled over their doorways. At the Last Supper the Lord explained how He was the Lamb whose body and blood would become eternally marked over God's people, bringing eternal salvation from the judgment of sin. As the Lamb, He both fulfilled the requirements of the first covenant and inaugurated the new covenant:

> *When He had taken some bread and given thanks, He broke it and gave it to them, saying, "This is My body which is given for you; do this in remembrance of Me." And in the same way He took the cup after they had eaten,*

saying, "This cup which is poured out for you is the new covenant in My blood" (Luke 22:19-20).

The idea that God intended to make another covenant with His people was not actually new. The prophet Jeremiah prophesied it years earlier:

"For this is the covenant that I will make with the house of Israel after those days, says the Lord: I will put My laws in their mind and write them on their hearts; and I will be their God, and they shall be My people. None of them shall teach his neighbor, and none his brother, saying, 'Know the Lord,' for all shall know Me, from the least of them to the greatest of them. For I will be merciful to their unrighteousness, and their sins and their lawless deeds I will remember no more." In that He says, "A new covenant," He has made the first obsolete. Now what is becoming obsolete and growing old is ready to vanish away (Hebrews 8: 10-13 NKJV).

To Jews, both in the first century and today, this passage is shocking and revolutionary. To say that the Old Covenant is obsolete and disappearing is akin to announcing that the Constitution of the United States of America is being completely dissolved and an entirely new system of government is being inaugurated. Every believer must feel the impact of this dramatic shift. The Law no longer defines the way in which we connect to God or God relates to us. The old contract is no longer enforced and has become irrelevant to the Kingdom.

In the New Covenant, the law is something we have in our hearts. This moves our focus from keeping rules to having a heart for the Lord. Only when we have God's law *written in our hearts* and our minds can we live with the extreme love that Jesus described in the Sermon on the Mount.

In the New Covenant, *God is merciful to us and remembers our sins no more.* Again, we need to comprehend this as a change of attitude in the Almighty. The Cross released us from judgment so

God could deal with us from the Mercy Seat. We were hidden in the Trojan horse of Christ.

The Cross of Christ brought us into Graceland! We didn't deserve to come in. We didn't qualify under the Law. We didn't get in through our own power, but instead we were hidden in the Trojan horse of Christ, which was wheeled into this new territory by the Cross (see Col. 3:3).

We were hidden in the Trojan horse of Christ.

What do I mean by Graceland? Graceland is the place where the people of God live far above the Law through the power of grace the New Covenant provided. Graceland is the Canaan of our souls. It is the place where there is no judgment. It is a Kingdom of love and forgiveness, a land of mercy and truth. *While there is discipline in this Kingdom, there is no punishment.*

JESUS WAS JUDGED FOR US

It probably sounds bold to say that we get to live in a realm of life in which we don't experience judgment, especially since that is a subject that looms large throughout both the Old and New Testaments. I want to clarify what I mean. In the beginning of this chapter we looked at judgment through the eyes of the Old Covenant. So now let's see what judgment looks like in Graceland through the rose-colored glasses of the Blood of Jesus.

When we learn in Sunday School that Jesus died for our sins, what many of us don't realize is that He died to deliver us from the judgment those sins brought on us. This is the main point of the most famous verse in the Bible. You would be hard-pressed to find a Christian who couldn't quote John 3:16. But I hardly ever meet a believer who understands that this is a transitional Scripture, the verse on which all of history pivots. It is the *good* in the Good News!

For God so loved the world, that He gave His only begotten Son, that whoever believes in Him shall not perish, but have eternal life. For God did not send the Son into the world to judge the world, but that the world might be saved through Him (John 3:16-17).

Later, John quotes Jesus' own words on this fact:

If anyone hears my sayings and does not keep them, I do not judge him; for I did not come to judge the world, but to save the world (John 12:47).

Jesus goes on to add that the Father doesn't judge anyone either:

For not even the Father judges anyone, but He has given all judgment to the Son, so that all will honor the Son even as they honor the Father. He who does not honor the Son does not honor the Father who sent Him (John 5:22-23).

Perhaps the most powerful indication that Jesus didn't come to judge us lies not in what Jesus said but what He didn't say. Jesus quoted Isaiah 61 as the inaugural address that launched Him into His ministry, but made an intentional omission in His quote. The original prophecy says:

*The Spirit of the Lord God is upon me, because the Lord has anointed me to bring good news to the afflicted; He has sent me to bind up the brokenhearted, to proclaim liberty to captives and freedom to prisoners; to proclaim the favorable year of the Lord and **the day of vengeance of our God**; to comfort all who mourn* (Isaiah 61:1-2).

But Jesus said:

The Spirit of the Lord is upon Me, because He anointed Me to preach the gospel to the poor. He has sent me to proclaim release to the captives, and recovery of sight to the blind, to set free those who are oppressed, to proclaim the favorable year of the Lord (Luke 4:18-19).

Did you notice the New Testament version ends with "the favorable year of the Lord" and does not include the rest of the sentence, "the day of vengeance of our God"? I'd like to suggest that this omission was intentional because Jesus wasn't sent to declare the day of vengeance, but to proclaim salvation (the favorable year of the Lord) to the world.

The "favorable year of the Lord" is a clear reference to the Jewish year of Jubilee. It came every 50 years and it was the time when all debts were forgiven and all slaves were set free. What a wonderful picture of the Graceland of our lives—the realm the Body of Christ was brought into on the day of Pentecost, which also means "50." What a great "year" to be alive.

In another place, Jesus did say judgment is on the world, but He was specifically referring to the devil, the "god of this world," and his kingdom, not people. *"Now judgment is upon this world; now the ruler of this world will be cast out"* (John 12:31). Since the Cross dealt with the issue of punishment, the judgment we experience in the Kingdom is judgment in our favor. It is accomplished as the enemy and his works are destroyed, and our Father, the Judge, restores to us that which he has stolen, killed, and destroyed in our lives. This is what judgment looks like in the New Covenant.

JUDGMENT DAY

Let me be clear. There is a Judgment Day coming, a dispensational season change for all those who ignore the *days* of grace. The Book of Revelation makes this very obvious, being filled with page after page of judgments for all those who decide to step on the precious blood of Jesus. But all through the New Testament, references to this season of the world's judgment are always related to *a day*, not the *Last Days*. What I am trying to say is that there are epoch seasons in the Kingdom that change the way in which God relates to the people of the world. We are currently in the *Last Days*, not the *Last Day*.

Let's look at what the "good doctor" had to say about this subject. Luke writes:

> *Therefore having overlooked the times of ignorance, God is now declaring to men that all people everywhere should repent, because He has fixed a day in which He will judge the world in righteousness through a Man whom He has appointed, having furnished proof to all men by raising Him from the dead* (Acts 17:30-31).

Peter echoes Luke's words in his book:

> *But by His word the present heavens and earth are being reserved for fire, kept for the **day of judgment** and destruction of ungodly men* (2 Peter 3:7).

Jude also repeats this theme:

> *Angels who did not keep their own domain, but abandoned their proper abode, He has kept in eternal bonds under darkness for the **judgment of the great day*** (Jude 6).

I think the most provoking passage concerning the Day of Judgment is exciting because it does not concern itself with judging others but the way in which we judge ourselves. These verses will drive you into Graceland.

Paul writes in First Corinthians:

> *For I am conscious of nothing against myself, yet I am not by this acquitted; but the one who examines me is the Lord. Therefore do not go on **passing judgment before the time**, but wait until the Lord comes who will both bring to light the things hidden in the darkness and disclose the motives of men's hearts; and then each man's praise will come to him from God* (1 Corinthians 4:4-5).

Paul is saying that he is unaware of anything wrong in himself, *but* admits he could still be messed up and not know it! He then explains that when the Day of Judgment comes, God will turn

His spotlight on the hearts of men and reveal the inner courts of their souls. But until Judgment Day, we don't have an accurate picture of what is going on in our own hearts, much less someone else's! He ends this verse with a powerful but almost hidden exhortation. He describes the "time of judgment" specifically as a time in which we will receive praise from God Himself. We spend our lives praising God on this earth, but on the final day when we get judged through the blood of Christ from the Mercy Seat, God will praise us. Now that rocks!

MERCY WHIPS JUDGMENT

When the reality of God's mercy, the fact that we no longer face any punishment for our sins, truly penetrates our souls, there is a simple and natural response that we express through our lives. We extend mercy. This is our royal, priestly ministry in the Kingdom of Grace. As Proverbs 19:11 states, *"A man's discretion makes him slow to anger, and it is his glory to overlook a transgression."* This word "discretion" means "understanding." Our understanding of mercy enables us to partake of the glory that only comes when we extend mercy to those around us.

James has some real insight into how we are practically to live in Graceland.

> *If, however, you are fulfilling the royal law according to the Scripture, "You shall love your neighbor as yourself," you are doing well. But if you show partiality, you are committing sin and are convicted by the law as transgressors. For whoever keeps the whole law and yet stumbles in one point, he has become guilty of all. For He who said, "Do not commit adultery," also said, "Do not commit murder." Now if you do not commit adultery, but do commit murder, you have become a transgressor of the law. So speak and so act as those who are to be judged by the law of liberty. For judgment will be merciless to one who has shown no mercy; mercy triumphs over judgment* (James 2:8-13).

James says showing partiality is stepping out of love and into law. But look at what he means by "showing partiality." This may surprise you. He explains to us that comparing sins—calling one sin worse than another—is showing partiality and makes us judges. He reminds us that when we make judgments about sin in people's lives we get deported back to the old country, where we are still fugitives wanted for the crimes committed against humanity.

I am personally amazed by how free believers and Christian leaders often seem to be to pronounce judgment against other people. It is common to hear believers make reference to a particular sin and call for judgment against cities or people groups that are participating in the sin they deem the worst. But they ignore the fact that although we have the responsibility to judge between right and wrong, we don't have the role, place, or responsibility to call for punishment against people. When we say homosexuality is worse than bitterness, or pornography is more sinful than gossip, we make ourselves judges of the Law and put ourselves under the merciless microscope of the Old Covenant. We had better watch out, because we are about to become the next victim of judgment. Remember, *nobody ever*, in the history of the planet, was found righteous under the Law except Jesus.

FLYING THE FRIENDLY SKIES

The other day I was awakened to the fact that I often judge people by the nature of their sin and exile them to the land of the untouchables without even getting to know them. Kathy and I were on a plane and we had not gotten seats together. She had a great aisle seat, so I asked the man sitting next to me, who was stuck in the middle seat, if he would like to swap seats with my wife. He immediately answered, "No!"

A minute later I noticed, out of the corner of my eye, that he was holding hands with the man next to him. Soon these two well-built, burly men in their 40s were boldly rubbing each other's arm and leg.

Yuck! I thought. *I am going to be sitting next to homosexuals for five hours.* I was getting angry and totally disgusted as these men romantically embraced each other. The longer we flew the more indignant I got. The funny thing is, I have sat next to hundreds of people who were into all kinds of sin over the years—people who were living together without being married, adulterers, liars, bitter folks, drunkards, drug addicts, and more—but I have never minded sitting next to them. This was different because I had judged these men. I had condemned them as unredeemable and had already decided that they should be punished.

As I sat there brewing, the Holy Spirit began to remind me that He loved these men. He was on a mission to draw them into the Kingdom and He needed someone to show them the heart of the King. I was reading a Christian book they had undoubtedly noticed. I turned to the guy next to me and introduced myself. "Hi, I'm Kris," I said, in a slightly guarded tone.

"Hi, I'm Frank," he responded, acting put out.

I looked over at his friend and introduced myself to him. He seemed angry, militant, and distant, but he said, "I'm Tony."

I offered them some cashews, showing them my muscles to let them view the results of my diet. They laughed. Tony said, "I'll take some."

Soon we were sharing food and exchanging laughs. Tony seemed to be staring at my book entitled *Building an Emotionally Healthy Church*. I could tell he was uncomfortable with it.

"Tony," I said jokingly, "You need this book!"

"I don't like the Church," he responded. "Those people scare me."

"Yeah, they scare me too, but they pay me to work there," I said, teasing him.

As the flight wore on we started to get to know each other. Tony was a CPA who hated his job and Frank was a helicopter pilot who flew for a hospital. I actually started to enjoy their company.

About an hour before we landed I began to get a prophetic word for Tony. "Tony, sometimes God gives me visions for people and I have one for you. Can I give it to you?" I asked.

"I guess," he said, obviously bracing himself for the worst.

"Tony, I saw you by the ocean with an easel, painting ocean-scapes and landscapes. Then the scene changed and you were sculpting and working with clay. Tony, God told me to tell you that He has really gifted you in the arts and He says He created you to make a living at it."

Before I could continue, Frank was freaking out, "Wow! That's absolutely true about Tony! He is an amazing artist and he loves to go to the ocean and paint the seashore."

Tony could hardly contain himself. He said, "I just took up sculpting and working with clay...wow! How encouraging."

We flew along for a little while longer and I could feel Frank's curiosity growing. I let him sweat a little. Then I said, "Frank, I have a word from God for you also."

Before I could ask him if I could give it to him, he said, "Oh good! Please give it to me."

"Frank, I see you fixing things. God has given you the uncanny ability to know what is wrong with mechanical things. You can fix anything. You love to work on things—you were born for this."

He was beaming, and Tony, who had gone from militant to open and impressed, said, "Frank, that is so you. You can repair anything!"

I learned so much on the plane that day—mercy finally had a victory in my life. And Tony and Frank were introduced to the Kingdom through a violent act of grace!

THE MINISTRY OF RECONCILIATION

Love and mercy are the core values of Heaven. We have to keep the values of the King when we minister in power, or we will be destructive instead of constructive. Paul made an amazing observation in the Book of Second Corinthians on this very subject.

> *Therefore if anyone is in Christ, he is a new creature; the old things passed away; behold, new things have come. Now all these things are from God, who reconciled us to Himself through Christ and gave us the ministry of reconciliation, namely, that God was in Christ reconciling the world to Himself, not counting their trespasses against them, and He has committed to us the word of reconciliation. Therefore, we are ambassadors for Christ, as though God were making an appeal through us; we beg you on behalf of Christ, be reconciled to God. He made Him who knew no sin to be sin on our behalf, so that we might become the righteousness of God in Him* (2 Corinthians 5:17-21).

This is an incredible revelation. God was in Christ so that He could reconcile the world to Himself. How did He reconcile the world to Himself? By "not counting their sins against them"! Did you get that? But as powerful as this is He also went on to say He has given us the *same* ministry. He wants us not to count sin against sinners so we can beg them to be reconciled to God. If God is not counting sin against sinners, what gives us the right to do it? And what ever gave us the idea that pointing out people's sin leads to reconciliation? God said *not* counting sins leads

God reconciled the world to Himself.

to reconciliation. We need to rethink the way in which we minister from the King's palace so we don't defile His throne and undermine His ministry. God reconciled the world to Himself.

MY JOURNEY TO GRACELAND

I say this with urgency because I have seen the damage caused, not only by the self-commissioned prophets of judgment I mentioned at the beginning of the chapter, but by a prophet I know well—me. When I lived in Weaverville I went to a church called Mountain Chapel, where Danny Silk was the senior pastor. One week Danny preached a message about offense and forgiveness in the Body of Christ. At the end of his message he told the people that if they had something against anyone in the room they needed to go to them right now and reconcile. There were about 200 people in the room that morning. I looked around and saw nobody going to anyone. Then I looked behind me and to my complete surprise, saw a line of people extending out the front door of the building and leading up to my seat. They were all waiting to talk to me. One by one they told me of the destruction I had caused in their lives over many years through my prophetic ministry. It wasn't a movie or bad dream—it was my prophetic ministry.

It was painful as they recounted scenes that sounded like battle sequences from the movie *Star Wars*. But it wasn't a movie, nor was it a bad dream. No, it was my prophetic ministry. My prophetic words were almost always accurate, but were destructive, harsh, and given in the wrong spirit. I had made it my practice to call out people's sins, and it mattered not that I struggled with some of the same things. Not only were my words negative; I would often share them in church or in a group of people. I had no idea how I was affecting the people I loved. That afternoon, somewhere around 3 P.M., I finally figured it out. I sat there for nearly three hours as I painfully and tearfully heard each person's offense until it finally occurred to me that something wasn't right in me! I received what we affectionately call a "revelation bump."

*I finally figured out that prophetic ministry, like every other ministry in the Kingdom, should be the love language of God. There's a reason that First Corinthians 13—the most important exhortation on love in the entire Bible—is sandwiched between the main chapters on the gifts of the Spirit. Every expression of the gifts of the Spirit should come from love and work to bring the love of the Father to the person receiving them. That is what the supernatural ministry of the New Covenant is all about. Love **never** fails!*

> *It wasn't a movie or bad dream—it was my prophetic ministry.*

CHAPTER 6

Cursing Christians

I want to take some time to expose the faulty foundations of a prophetic ministry carried out with an Old Testament paradigm. I talked about prophetic judgments in my first book *The Supernatural Ways of Royalty*. But this subject is so important and so misunderstood in our day that I felt compelled to share some of the same perspective in a different setting here. As I have mentioned, there are many prophetic people who are convinced that their main ministry is to warn people of the coming judgments of God. Although the Lord does give prophetic warnings for impending disasters, *blaming* God for calamity is quite a different thing. Let's take a closer look at the facts and fallacies of prophetic declarations. The Lord gives prophetic warnings but is not to blame for calamities.

Agabus was a New Testament prophet who saw disaster ahead and warned the people of God:

> *Now at this time some prophets came down from Jerusalem to Antioch. One of them named Agabus stood up and*

> *began to indicate by the Spirit that there would certainly be a great famine all over the world. And this took place in the reign of Claudius* (Acts 11:27-28).

It is important to note that Agabus didn't blame God for the famine nor did he relate the calamity to someone's sin. Connecting natural disasters with the sins of the people of the land was often the main message of Old Testament prophets. But Agabus didn't do that. He wasn't blaming God for the famine; he was simply trying to prepare the Body of Christ for the trouble he saw ahead.

There is an amazing testimony of God's saving grace in Central America through a prophetic warning vision. In 1976, a woman from Guatemala had a vision of great destruction coming to her country. She predicted that an earthquake would happen within the first four or five days of February, about four months from the day she had the vision. She submitted the prophetic vision to her leaders. They prayed about it and discerned that the vision was from God. In response, the church members humbled themselves before God and cried out for mercy. Then they slept outside for the first few days of February. The leaders told government officials about the vision, but they didn't heed their warning.

At 3:02 A.M. on the morning of February 4, 1976, one of the deadliest earthquakes in recent history shook Guatemala, killing over 22,000 people and injuring about 74,000. Measuring 7.5 on the Richter scale, it destroyed entire cities, leaving one million people homeless. Remarkably, the churches did not lose a single person.

The Lord gives prophetic warnings but is not to blame for calamities.

Norman Parish, who was the leader of the churches, began a private relief program, which is reported to be the largest in Latin American history. When the government saw the awesome job Norman's team was doing, they loaned him whatever he needed to help with the relief effort. They even gave him helicopters and assigned the national army to feed his relief teams.

THE SOURCE OF NATURAL DISASTERS

This is probably a good time to discuss the laws and workings of nature. Earthquakes, tornadoes, famines, hurricanes, and even old age aren't necessarily acts of God or the devices of the devil. (Earthquakes, for example, are simply the sudden release of tectonic stress along a fault line.) To relate every calamity to the spirit realm is simply ignorant and results in Christians losing credibility with anybody who has permission to think. I do understand that the spirit realm can and does have preeminence over the material realm, but God also created the laws of nature, which perpetuate without His intervention. When we prophesy from a core value that God causes all natural disasters, we teach pre-Christians to blame God for everything that goes wrong in the world. Even insurance companies have coined the phrase "acts of God" when referring to natural disasters that they won't insure. But the Bible has a much different paradigm for this.

JUSTICE HAS BEEN SERVED

As we discussed in the previous chapter, the wrath of God was poured out on Jesus at the Cross, bringing justice and releasing mercy to billions of people who don't deserve it. Therefore God doesn't need to create justice through judgment, because He already did that in the person of Jesus.

Clearly there are still times when God's love and wisdom cause Him to remove people from the earth, as He did in the case of Ananias and Sapphira. It is interesting to note that Peter was talking to Ananias about lying when Ananias fell dead. I doubt Peter knew that Ananias was going to die just for lying. After all, Peter is among the most famous liars in the Bible. He lied about knowing Jesus, a slightly more important subject than how much a piece of land was sold for. But by the time Sapphira came into the room, Peter figured out that God had decided to take them home early and he said to her, *"Why is it that you have agreed together to put the Spirit of the Lord to the test? Behold, the feet of those who have buried your husband are at the door, and they will carry you out as well"* (Acts 5:9).

An angel in the Book of Acts killed King Herod (without anybody prophesying against him) because he allowed people to worship him instead of God (see Acts 12:23). Of course, the moral to this story is, "Be nice to your angel!" (Just joking.) It is important to note that God did not kill Herod for arresting His apostles and trying to execute them but because he stole God's glory. The point is that the Lord is God and He can do whatever He wants to do, *but He doesn't need to bring judgment to create justice.*

There would be a lot of dead people in the Church today if God chose to employ the standard He used on Ananias, Sapphira, and Herod as His normal response to sin! If you think these Scriptures give you permission to prophesy judgment against people, you had better ask yourself if you have ever lied or received credit from men that wasn't yours but God's. I think we would have a huge depopulation of the planet if this were God's usual reaction to transgressions.

> *Pharisees love to point out the sins of others.*
>
> ❧

We will not get God to stay in any theological box no matter how tightly we seal the cracks with our doctrines, but we can know the heart of our Lord so we understand how He thinks. James puts it this way:

Every good thing given and every perfect gift is from above, coming down from the Father of lights with whom there is no variation or shifting shadow (James 1:17).

How many people have died, been mangled or maimed, broken, raped, or made destitute in the name of God without Him ever being involved? When is the Church going to start presenting Jesus as a loving God? So much of the prophetic movement is misrepresenting the heart of the King.

AN ANGRY GOD?

Judgment words represent our heavenly Father as a Person who has only one response to the sins and the problems of the world—kill everybody! I have heard many prophecies from famous prophets who believe God is judging America for the millions of abortions that we, as a nation, have committed. But think about this core value. Does it make any sense to you to say that God is so mad about people taking the lives of their own children that He is going to show them the error of their way by killing millions more people? It is true that our Father is grieved over the multitude of babies who are being slaughtered daily on the altar of convenience. But the ultimate reason most mothers are taking the lives of their own children is that they don't understand the love of God. Representing God as an angry Being is only compounding the problem.

If your 16-year-old daughter got pregnant and had an abortion without your knowing about it, only to confess it to you a couple months later, how would you respond? Would you want to kill her? If you answered affirmatively to this question, then you are a part of the reason she aborted her child. She didn't have anyone she could confide in to help her through this terrifying situation. A good father would have been grieved, both because his daughter killed her baby and because she didn't trust him enough to come to him when she was in trouble. We need to let the world know that the Father weeps over our nation's cold-hearted murder of its unborn. Pharisees love to point out the sins of others.

It's the religious spirit that rejoices in the punishment of sinners. Remember when the Pharisees caught the woman in the act of adultery? They exposed her transgression to everyone in town. Pharisees love to point out the sins of others because they get their sense of righteousness by catching others in their stuff. (You can always feel good about yourself depending on whom you compare yourself to). Look at the contrast between the attitude of the religious leaders and the response of Jesus:

> *The scribes and the Pharisees brought a woman caught in adultery, and having set her in the center of the court, they said to Him, "Teacher, this woman has been caught in adultery, in the very act. Now in the Law Moses commanded us to stone such women; what then do You say?" They were saying this, testing Him, so that they might have grounds for accusing Him. But Jesus stooped down and with His finger wrote on the ground. But when they persisted in asking Him, He straightened up, and said to them, "He who is without sin among you, let him be the first to throw a stone at her." Again He stooped down and wrote on the ground. When they heard it, they began to go out one by one, beginning with the older ones, and He was left alone, and the woman, where she was, in the center of the court. Straightening up, Jesus said to her, "Woman, where are they? Did no one condemn you?" She said, "No one, Lord." And Jesus said, "I do not condemn you, either. Go. From now on sin no more"* (John 8:3-11).

Let's leave the pharisaical spirit behind and embrace the love of God that covers sins. We will gain some more insight into this story later in this book.

DISASTER LEADS TO REVIVAL?

Many folks believe that disasters in people's lives humble them and cause them to be open to the gospel. They reason that if disaster leads to repentance then the end justifies the means. But this entire way of thinking is flawed. I would like to point out to you that every Christian knows people who are angry with God because they had a child, a spouse, a parent, or a friend die an untimely death. The disaster drove them away from our Savior, not closer. For every person who has found God in a crash, there are ten "walking wounded" who wander the earth wondering how a loving God could allow such terrible things to happen to the innocent. This truth is exemplified throughout the Bible. Check out the attitudes of Korah's tribe when God killed Korah for his rebellion against Moses. Here is the account:

> *The earth opened its mouth and swallowed them up, and their households, and all the men who belonged to Korah with their possessions...But on the next day all the congregation of the sons of Israel grumbled against Moses and Aaron, saying, "You are the ones who have caused the death of the Lord's people"* (Numbers 16:32,41).

Hardly a repentant attitude, I would say. How about the repentant attitude of those who are caught in the tribulations of the Last Days? Look at this:

> *Then the fifth angel poured out his bowl on the throne of the beast, and his kingdom became darkened; and they gnawed their tongues because of pain, and they blasphemed the God of heaven because of their pains and their sores; and they did not repent of their deeds* (Revelation 16:10-11).

The truth is that tragedy doesn't necessarily lead people to God. Furthermore, most revivals throughout history were not the result of worldly trouble but the manifestation of a sovereign move of God. The Azusa Street revival that swept the entire earth wasn't the result of a calamity. Neither was the Charismatic movement or the Jesus movement inspired by catastrophe. The Welsh revival was not the result of trouble. The most recent Toronto outpouring was actually a revival that began as a revelation of the goodness of the Father. People laughed and cried as they experienced the amazing love of Jesus.

On the other hand, America experienced a major crisis in the terrorist attack of September 11, 2001. Many churches filled up for a few months, but when the scare was over it was back to business as usual for the United States. You may be able to scare a few people into the Kingdom with doom and gloom, but you can't keep them there with these tactics, because there is no fear in the Kingdom of Love.

LIFE AND DEATH ARE IN THE POWER OF THE TONGUE

Some time ago I was in a conference where a prophet spoke publicly about a disaster coming to a certain city on Friday. It was Wednesday night. Friday morning we woke to the news of the very tragedy the prophet had spoken of. It happened just as he said it would. At the Friday conference session, he got up and quoted the newspaper article. Most of the people were there on Wednesday when he made his prophetic declaration. The people stood and applauded. I was so angry! After the session I drove him back to his room. On the way there I asked him why he let the people of God celebrate the death of so many. Somebody's daughter died, someone's mother, someone's father, someone's son, someone's baby—you get the idea. Perhaps our "nameless and faceless" value system is working against the love we once had for individuals who all used to have names and faces. It is so easy to prophesy against people you can't see or don't know.

> The more authority you carry in Christ the great the impact.
>
> ❧

But somebody loves all of these people; at the very least God loves them. Many would ask, "If God loves these people then why did He destroy them?" The answer is that He didn't! Let me explain.

"Death and life are in the power of the tongue" (Prov. 18:21). The more authority you carry in Christ, the greater the impact your words have.

The confusion lies in the fact that some folks believe if you can cause something to happen through a prophetic proclamation, then God initiated the declaration. This is simply not true. *"The gifts and the calling of God are irrevocable"* (Rom. 11:29). People use the gifts of God for their own personal gain every day. Just as people can control the natural gifts

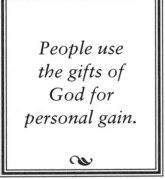

People use the gifts of God for personal gain.

and abilities God gives them, they can also control and manipulate the spiritual gifts He gives. There are numerous examples of this principle throughout the Scriptures. The more authority you carry in Christ the great the impact.

One of the clearest examples of this is in the life of King Saul. When God rejected him from being king, the presence of the Lord withdrew from him and God refused to talk to him. Saul got really desperate to hear from God and went to see the witch at Endor. He asked her to call Samuel, the prophet, up from the dead. It is important to understand that Scripture strictly forbids calling up anyone from the dead, much less conjuring up a prophet. But Samuel came up from the dead anyway and spoke to Saul (see 1 Sam. 28:7-25). (Some people say that it was a demon that looked like Samuel. But the Bible is unapologetic about the fact that it was clearly Samuel.) The point I am trying to make here is that the witch caused a prophet to come back from the dead even though it wasn't the will of God. People use the gifts of God for personal gain.

How about this story of the irritable prophet who destroyed 42 young boys with his curses:

> *Then [Elisha] went up from there to Bethel; and as he was going up by the way, young lads came out from the city and mocked him and said to him, "Go up, you baldhead; go up, you baldhead!" When he looked behind him and saw*

> Don't allow the enemy access to our mighty weapons of warfare.
>
> ∾

them, he cursed them in the name of the Lord. Then two female bears came out of the woods and tore up forty-two lads of their number (2 Kings 2:23-24).

Do you really think that God wanted 42 young boys to be torn up just because they teased a prophet? I doubt it! Elisha used his power to punish the kids who teased him, not because it was the will of God but because it was the will of the prophet.

Much like these people who used their spiritual power for their own gain, a prophet or prophetic people can declare an earthquake or some kind of disaster and have it come to pass, but it doesn't validate that their word was inspired by God. It simply means that the one who prophesied it carries a lot of power in the unseen realm. This is one of the most misunderstood and yet significant truths of the Kingdom. Believers have much authority in the spirit realm. Unrealized, this authority can become destructive instead of constructive.

AGREEING WITH THE ACCUSER

The devil is called the accuser of the brethren, so it shouldn't surprise us that there is so much negativity in the world. Here is how the apostle John put it:

> Then I heard a loud voice in heaven, saying, "Now the salvation, and the power, and the kingdom of our God and the authority of His Christ have come, for the accuser of our brethren has been thrown down, he who accuses them before our God day and night (Revelation 12:10).

The devil has been cast down from Heaven and no longer has access to God. So how does he accuse people before God day and night? He sends Christians, who do have access to the throne, to do his dirty work for him! We make agreements with his accusations and release curses on people. It is extremely important that the mighty weapons of our warfare don't fall into the hands of the enemy and destroy the very people we are supposed to be preserving. Don't allow the enemy access to our mighty weapons of warfare.

A famous university recently did a research project that really drives this point home. What their study uncovered was stunning. The average person subconsciously hears 1,200 words a minute of self-talk. Eleven hundred of those words are negative in most people! It is no wonder the devil is called the prince of the power of the air. Think about what he is putting out over the airwaves—destructive junk that disempowers and defaces the very people who were made in the image of God. This is why so many people commit suicide and a staggering number of people are on anti-depressant drugs.

Break all agreements with the accuser!

Prophetic people, let's break all agreements with the accuser and stop doing his dirty work for him! Break all agreements with the accuser!

CHAPTER 7

Keeping Secrets

We took a look at core values and the effect they have on our worldview. We also examined the difference between the ministry of the Old and New Testaments and saw the destructive nature of wrong prophetic paradigms. Now let's talk about the different ways we process prophecy in Graceland as we look through the Son-glasses of the Kingdom of God.

PASTORING SUPERNATURAL MINISTRY

A few months ago I had just finished preaching in our Sunday morning first service and I was getting ready to begin the second service. A lady in her mid-fifties approached me as I was walking to the pulpit. I was a few minutes late getting the second service started, so I was feeling a little rushed.

"I have a word from the Lord for you," she said with a smile. She could see I was hurrying so she said, "It will just take a minute."

"Okay," I said, looking at my watch and hoping it wouldn't take long. I bowed my head and closed my eyes to try to concentrate in the midst of all the hustle.

She spoke something over me, which to this day I can't remember. Then, to my surprise, she poured something on my head! My eyes were still closed and I could feel something like cold shampoo running down my hair. Suddenly I opened my eyes as she proclaimed, "God told me to pour this oil on your head."

I couldn't believe it! She poured an entire flask of oil on my head. Oil was running off my hair and onto my nice shirt. Kevin, one of our pastors, turned to me and, laughing his head off, said, "If I were you, I would go to the restroom before you go to the pulpit."

I was so mad! I went to the bathroom to try to wash it out of my hair, but it was no use. My wife was somewhere else during the incident and didn't know what had happened. She entered the sanctuary while I was still opening the service. When I returned to my seat she looked at me and said, "What did you do to your hair? You look like Elvis!"

There are a lot of things done in the name of God, many of which are embarrassing at best, and at worst are downright destructive. If we are going to cultivate a supernatural lifestyle, there must be accountability for the things that are done in the Lord's name. Prophecy is one of the gifts of the Spirit that needs to be pastored. People who move in the spiritual gifts should expect and invite the scrutiny of their ministry. When poor or bad supernatural ministry goes unchecked or unchallenged by other mature believers, it creates a culture where people lose faith in the miraculous. But when we develop a culture that expects supernatural ministry to be evaluated, not with a critical eye but with the discerning wisdom of mature believers, we produce a safety net that young disciples can grow in.

Anyone who refuses to yield their supernatural ministry to mature leaders should not be allowed to minister to the Body.

Phrases like, "The Lord compelled me to say this" or "God told me I had to do that" are simply inexcusable. The Bible says, "The spirit of the prophet is subject to the prophet" (see 1 Cor. 14:32). This means that we are responsible to manage the gifts of the Spirit that operate in and through our lives. This is why one of fruits of the Spirit is *self-control* (see Gal. 5:23). We have the responsibility to control ourselves.

THE DIFFERENCE BETWEEN OLD AND NEW TESTAMENT PROPHECY

All prophecy needs to be judged, but there is a huge difference between judging Old and New Testament prophecy. Part of this is due to the way in which the prophets of old heard from God, and the way in which we hear from the Lord today. In the Old Testament, prophets *received* the word of the Lord. In the New Testament, prophetic people *perceive* the word of the Lord. In the Old Testament, the Spirit of God did not live inside of mankind, nor was the spirit of man resurrected. Our spirits weren't given life until we were born again. Therefore, when a prophet in the Old Testament heard from God, it was an *occasion* because Christ was not living inside of them.

The only method they had of judging Old Testament prophecy was to see if it came to pass, because the people who received these prophetic declarations were spiritually dead. They had no spiritual paradigm in which to process this Third Heaven information.

HERE IS THE OLD TESTAMENT PARADIGM FOR JUDGING PROPHECY:

When a prophet speaks in the name of the Lord, if the thing does not come about or come true, that is the thing which the Lord has not spoken. The prophet has spoken it presumptuously; you shall not be afraid of him (Deuteronomy 18:22).

It is easy to see why they killed Old Testament prophets who misled them. These men had tremendous influence over people, countries, and kingdoms. It is important to note that people who disobeyed their prophets and priest were also killed.

A HOUSE FOR TWO

In this new dispensation, our spirit is alive and the Holy Spirit also lives inside us. In other words, our body has actually become home to two spirits, our spirit and the Holy Spirit. It is easy to get the Holy Spirit's words confused with our newly regenerated spirit's words because our spirit didn't just come alive; it also took on the "divine nature" (2 Pet. 1:4). No longer is it only the Holy Spirit that wants to build people up in Christ, but our spirit is now inherently good and very much wants to bless people also. You can see how in our zeal to help and encourage people, we can represent a word as a God idea when it is actually only a good idea. Thus, in the New Testament Church, the Christian who receives a prophetic word has as much responsibility to judge the word as the one who gave it, because both the giver and receiver have the same Holy Spirit living inside them. Our body is home to two spirits—our spirit and the Holy Spirit.

> *Our body is home to two spirits—our spirit and the Holy Spirit.*

JUDGING PROPHETIC WORDS IN THE NEW TESTAMENT

Paul writes, *"Let two or three prophets speak, and let the others pass judgment"* (1 Cor. 14:29). Notice that the prophetic word is to be judged immediately. What exactly are we judging when we are examining prophetic words? Obviously the first thing we are trying to determine is the source of the word. Is it from God's Spirit, the human spirit, or from a demonic spirit? But how can we judge a prophecy when it is about the future? The Holy Spirit who lives within us can discern the validity in the word and bear witness to our spirit, because He is supposed to be the source of all prophetic declarations.

There are a few other principles that will help us to distinguish which words are from the Lord:

✧ The word must be congruent with the Scriptures as well as the heart of Father God. Paul writes:

But even if we, or an angel from heaven, should preach to you a gospel contrary to what we have preached to you, he is to be accursed! (Galatians 1:8)

✧ A prophetic word must bear witness with the spirit of the one who receives it. It doesn't necessarily have to make sense to our minds, but there must be a *"yes"* in our spirits.

✧ The fruit of all prophetic words must be that the person receiving it is brought closer to God and His people. Prophetic words that separate people from the Body of Christ do not find their source in God.

✧ The prophets and the church leadership should be in agreement with the word and its interpretation and application. When God gives leaders oversight in our lives, He also gives them insight into our lives. They will often see things in us and have perspectives about us that no one else has. Here's what the author of the Book of Hebrews has to say about our leaders:

Obey your leaders and submit to them, for they keep watch over your souls as those who will give an account. Let them do this with joy and not with grief, for this would be unprofitable for you (Hebrews 13:17).

✧ The interpretation of any prophetic revelation belongs to God, not to man. Therefore we also need the Holy Spirit's anointing to know the meaning of the word as well as what to do with it. Peter wrote this:

But know this first of all, that no prophecy of Scripture is a matter of one's own interpretation, for no prophecy was ever made by an act of human will, but men moved by the Holy Spirit spoke from God (2 Peter 1:20-21).

PROPHETIC WORDS UNDERSTOOD
AFTER THE FACT

There are times when we receive a prophetic word and don't realize what it means until *after* it has been fulfilled. An example of this is found in Exodus 3, where Moses asked God for a sign so he could know for sure that it was God who was sending him. The Lord spoke to him and said, "After you bring the people out of Egypt, you will worship at this mountain."

"Therefore, come now, and I will send you to Pharaoh, so that you may bring My people, the sons of Israel, out of Egypt." But Moses said to God, "Who am I, that I should go to Pharaoh, and that I should bring the sons of Israel out of Egypt?" And He said, "Certainly I will be with you, and this shall be the sign to you that it is I who have sent you: when you have brought the people out of Egypt, you shall worship God at this mountain" (Exodus 3:10-12).

Likewise, Jesus' prophecy of His own death and resurrection wasn't understood until after He rose from the dead.

Jesus answered them, "Destroy this temple, and in three days I will raise it up." The Jews then said, "It took forty-six years to build this temple, and will You raise it up in three days?" But He was speaking of the temple of His body. So when He was raised from the dead, His disciples remembered that He said this; and they believed the Scripture and the word, which Jesus had spoken (John 2:19-22).

WATCHING THE CLOCK

Then there is the issue of timing. Every prophetic person needs to ask, in every instance, "Is this the right time and circumstance to share this word?" Proverbs puts it this way, *"Like apples of gold in settings of silver is a word spoken in right circumstances"* (Prov. 25:11). Bad timing can put our golden apples in a very awkward setting. I had a humorous experience that made this come to life for me. I was in the men's restroom at a church in Montana and there was a picture of a beautiful waterfall hanging over the urinal. It had a caption under it that read, *"When you pass through the water I will be with you."* It was a right word in a totally wrong setting!

> *A right word can be ruined by sharing it in the wrong setting or at the wrong time.*

Kathy and I have been married for 31 years. There are some things that happen between us as married people that must only take place in an appropriate setting for them to be right. Ministry is like that too. Sometimes a right word can be ruined by sharing it in the wrong setting or at the wrong time. A right word can be ruined by sharing it in the wrong setting or at the wrong time.

PURELY GOD?

I used to teach that prophetic ministry needed to be purely God and shouldn't have any humanity in it. I still believe that, but in a different way. I have come to realize that the Lord is so brilliant. He knows how to arrange the circumstances so the person with a certain personality type, a particular life experience, and a specific doctrinal slant is divinely appointed to minister to a specific person who needs that exact mix. The truth is that there is really no way to get us out of our prophetic words, because as soon as we open our mouth, it sounds like us, looks like us, and it has our personality woven all through it. Not only can we not get ourselves out of our prophetic words, but even more importantly, *we* are a part of the prophetic word. We are a part of the prophetic word.

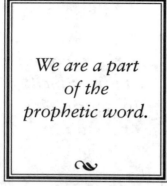

We are a part of the prophetic word.

We can see this principle working through the Old Testament prophets. Some prophets were farmers while others were called to politics or something else. Jeremiah was a softhearted guy, but Elijah was an impatient prophet whom you wouldn't want to cross. But God actually created them for a certain time, had them born to divinely appointed parents, put them in a specific place in history, and arranged for them to have unique life experiences so *they* would be part of the word!

Of course, I am not saying that God wants us consciously to put our stuff in His prophetic declarations. I am simply saying we can't keep ourselves out of our prophetic words because we don't know where God begins and we end.

When we join God in ministry and life, it is like pouring blue and red paint together. Suddenly you have the color purple. But try to separate the paint back to blue and red. We couldn't do it. That's the way it is with God and us—we are together forever, partners in destiny!

GETTING SOME OF IT RIGHT

It is possible for part of a particular prophetic word to be right and some of it to be wrong. Paul said, *"Do not quench the Spirit; do not despise prophetic utterances. But examine everything carefully; hold fast to that which is good"* (1 Thess. 5:19-21). Because prophecy is made of three parts, revelation, interpretation, and application, it isn't too hard to get the revelation right but get the interpretation and/or application wrong. It is easy to understand why Paul says, "Don't despise prophetic utterances." Remember what we talked about earlier—living in the Spirit is risky business.

Some time ago, a team of us traveled to a conference where they were training people how to prophesy. I had an amazing experience there that taught me how easy it is to get a prophetic revelation right and get the interpretation totally wrong.

The leaders of the conference broke us up into classes of about 70 people. Someone from the conference was brought to the front and we were to give them ten prophetic words and then have the recipient judge the words we gave them. In this particular instance, we were all prophesying to a middle-aged gal whom the leader picked to be our "guinea pig." When we had completed the prophecies, she began the process of judging the words that were given to her. In the midst of judging the words, a man in the back of the room stood to his feet and yelled, "You have on a yellow shirt!"

Immediately the woman fell to the ground, crying hysterically. The man continued to prophesy things like, "The sun is yellow. The moon is yellow." When the woman finally regained her composure, the leader of the class asked what the word meant to her. She explained, "I have a son who is autistic and I told the Lord today, 'If you are going to heal my son, have someone tell me that I have on a yellow shirt.'"

The prophetic word had nothing to do with how the color yellow related to the sun or moon. It was strictly a sign the lady asked the Lord for. But the man got nervous and began to try to make the word mean something else. He didn't understand that the word was simply a sign of God's agreement to heal the lady's son.

SELECTIVE HEARING

It is easy to misjudge a prophetic word by believing that it relates to our *immediate* circumstances or something close to our heart that we are hoping for. This is called *selective hearing*. Sometimes people simply hear what they want to hear. I have given thousands of prophetic words to people over the years and I am amazed at what people *think* they heard me say sometimes. Occasionally, what the person hears me prophesy to them is not even

> *Sometimes people hear what they want to hear.*

close to the word I gave them! Sometimes people hear what they want to hear.

Matthew 16 provides a vivid example of this sort of misinterpretation:

Jesus said to them, "Watch out and beware of the leaven of the Pharisees and Sadducees." They began to discuss this among themselves, saying, "He said that because we did not bring any bread." But Jesus, aware of this, said, "You men of little faith, why do you discuss among yourselves that you have no bread? Do you not yet understand or remember the five loaves of the five thousand, and how many baskets full you picked up? Or the seven loaves of the four thousand, and how many large baskets full you picked up? How is it that you do not understand that I did not speak to you concerning bread? But beware of the leaven of the Pharisees and Sadducees." Then they understood that He did not say to beware of the leaven of bread, but of the teaching of the Pharisees and Sadducees (Matthew 16:6-12).

The disciples had neglected to bring bread. (Their response is a telltale sign that they had a reputation for being irresponsible.) How did the disciples get the idea that Jesus was scolding them for forgetting to bring bread from the word, *"Beware of the leaven of the Pharisees and Sadducees?"* They read their circumstances into His word!

We live so much in the here and now, but God lives in the timeless zone. Our life goals are often based on getting out of pain or finding pleasure, but God is in the character building business. When we are stressed out about paying the electric bill, it is hard for us to imagine that God could be giving us a word that is for ten years into the future. We tend to think the Lord is feeling our pressure and is speaking to us about the thing we are stressed about. When we are in "deliver me from all my worries mode" it is easy to misinterpret prophetic declarations.

HOW TO RECEIVE PROPHETIC WORDS

When we get a prophetic word and we determine that it is from God, the next step is to learn how to receive it. It is important to know when to *get out of the way* and when to *prepare the way*. This point is illustrated in the life of Abraham and Sarah in Genesis 16–21. God told them that they were going to have a son. But the years rolled on and they still had no children. They decided to help God bring about the word in their life by having Abraham sleep with Hagar, Sarah's maid. This resulted in Hagar's giving birth to Ishmael. Ishmael persecuted Isaac, the child of promise, the rest of his days (see Gal. 4:29). It's important to know when to *get out* of the way and when *to prepare* the way.

> *It's important to know when to get out of the way and when to prepare the way.*
> ❧

Later on God came to Abraham and Sarah and prophesied to them that they would have a son the following year. Sarah laughed and said, *"After I have become old, shall I have pleasure, my lord being old also?"* (Gen. 18:12). But despite her doubt, Isaac was born the following year. The amazing thing to remember here is that Isaac was not conceived by the Holy Spirit like Jesus was. Abraham and Sarah had to be involved in the act of marriage to have Isaac. So on one hand they created an Ishmael by trying to make the prophetic word come to pass, but on the other hand, they still had to co-labor with God to see the promise become a reality. We need to realize that God seldom does anything all by Himself. He often requires us to be involved with Him to see our destinies fulfilled. The key here is to allow the Holy Spirit to show us what part He wants us to play and what part God has reserved for Himself. Otherwise we will create Ishmaels who will persecute our Isaacs!

> *Businesspeople often exchange the marketplace for the pulpit and preach to overfed folks.*
> ❧

There is a great story of an old farmer who had not been to church in a couple of weeks because he was in the middle of harvesting his orchard. After the second week his pastor came out to the farm to see him and encourage him to come back to church. The farmer explained his dilemma to his pastor but his pastor was unmoved.

The pastor said, "If you come to church God will take care of your fields for you!"

The old farmer directed the pastor to a large plot of ground that was overgrown with weeds. Pointing to the field he said, "See that field? That is the field I let God take care of by Himself!" God loves to co-labor with us.

RECEIVING PROPHETIC MINISTRY MULTI-DIMENSIONALLY

We also need to learn how to receive prophetic ministry multi-dimensionally. In other words, when God speaks to us about doing something new, He doesn't necessarily want us to stop doing the thing in which we are currently involved. Often He wants to add to that for which we are already responsible. This is illustrated in the parable of the talents. When the stewards were faithful with a few talents, they received more. They didn't lose the ones they had to get other ones. We need to be careful how we apply prophetic words to our lives because God wants to bless us abundantly.

I have watched business leaders, for instance, receive prophetic words that they were called to be pastors. Often it doesn't occur to them that their flock could be in the market-place. The marketplace is full of lost sheep that are starving for a true shepherd. But businesspeople often exchange the mar-ketplace for the pulpit and wind up preaching to folks who are already overfed. Businesspeople often exchange the market-place for the pulpit and preach to overfed folks.

DEVELOPING A REFUSE GATE

Some people are overly sensitive to negative spiritual experiences. Somebody gives them a bad word, and they act like they are ruined for life. So they spend their entire lives trying to stay safe and clean. But God has actually made His people pretty durable.

In the city of Jerusalem there was a refuse gate. This was the area where all of the city garbage was dumped. Our own human body has a system of elimination that disposes of anything we consume that does not nourish the body. Our spirit needs a system of elimination as well, lest we be poisoned by poor ministry or, worse yet, starved to death by those who refuse the Holy Spirit's work because they are afraid that somebody might "slime" them.

When we first came to Bethel, some on the ministry team didn't want to pray for certain people because they felt like they were picking up "hitchhikers" from them (a code word for evil spirits). I told them, "Jesus touched lepers and He didn't get leprosy, but the lepers got clean. If we only pray for people who are clean, how do the unclean get well?"

Besides that, the Bible says, *"Greater is He who is in you than he who is in the world"* (1 John 4:4). Evil spirits are no match for the God who lives inside us. The fear of getting "slimed" by those we are praying for is a commentary on us more than it is an evaluation of the folks who need to get free.

I am always reminded of this when folks from the occult come to hang out with us. A lot of witches come to our services because a few of their leaders have gotten saved in our church. They are usually there to harass them and throw curses at us. It freaks some of our people out and they want to fight with them or rebuke them. People who are caught up in witchcraft have great defenses

> *"Men are known...in Heaven by the secrets they keep."*

for cursing Christians. But they don't know what to do when we love on them and show them affection they don't deserve. Blessing people who curse us is a powerful way to live and it sends a message to the devil that he has messed with the wrong folks!

KEEPING SECRETS

Finally, not only do we need to judge the source of prophecy but we also need to discern if the word is supposed to be kept a secret or if it is all right for us to share it. The prophet Amos wrote, *"Surely the Lord God does nothing unless He reveals His secret counsel to His servants the prophets"* (Amos 3:7). It would be good for us to understand that all prophetic words begin as secrets. We need permission to share them. The prophet Bob Jones says, "Men are known on earth by the things they share but they are known in Heaven by the secrets they keep." "Men are known...in Heaven by the secrets they keep."

May we become friends of God who can be trusted with prophetic declarations that alter the course of world history.

CHAPTER 8

Mission Impossible

❧

OPEN VISIONS

It was a hot day in July, the kind when sweat pours from your head and you are desperate for shade. It was also the last day of a grueling youth outing where 35 high school kids and 3 of us leaders had been jammed into a 900-square-foot house for days. The kids, of course, were still full of energy, but I was frazzled. On this final day we had taken the youth group to the Santa Cruz Boardwalk for one final hurrah before we went home.

It happened to be muscle beach day at the boardwalk, and a bodybuilding contest was taking place on a large concrete platform rising out of the sandy beach. While the kids were riding the huge rollercoaster down by the water, I sat up against one of the four large pillars that supported the beach stage, trying to enjoy a few minutes of solace in the shadow of the platform. The beach was packed with sunbathers and their towels covering the hot sand looked like a large quilt. On the platform above me, the bodybuilding judges were yelling their decisions over the P.A. as spectators watched from the boardwalk about 50 yards from the stage. My tattered nerves were just beginning to unwind in spite of the chaos when my peace was suddenly shattered.

I glanced out to the water's edge and I noticed Dee running along the beach with a man in full black motorcycle leathers chasing her. Dee was our foster child, and though she was 15 years old, she had the emotions of a 12-year-old and the figure of a mature woman. She had evidently given up the roller-coaster ride to use her beautiful body to "troll" for men along the beach.

They were about a hundred yards away, with a sea of people separating us. I could tell he was yelling something while he ran after her, but I couldn't make out what he was saying. I struggled to my knees, gripped with concern. Dee was looking for help, and finally our eyes locked across the crowded sand. She turned and began to rush towards me with the motorcycle dude in tow. He was closing in on her, still shouting wildly as they ran over people lying on the beach. When they grew close, I could finally hear what he was saying.

"I love you! I am taking you with me!"

I was so scared that my body shook uncontrollably, my legs wobbled like a newborn colt, and my mouth felt filled with cotton. Dee dove to a spot next to me on my right, landing on her knees.

The young man reached down, grabbed her by the straps of her halter-top, lifted her from the sand, and yelled, "I love you! I love you! I am taking you with me! I am taking you with me!"

I was paralyzed with fear and couldn't move a muscle. A voice in my spirit yelled, "Tell him about Me! Tell him about Me!"

I protested, "God, I don't know if You noticed, but this man doesn't seem to be open to evangelism. He wants to hurt someone!"

But God kept forcefully pressing me, "Tell him about Me!"

My mind was racing but suddenly I grabbed his arm and yelled, "That is enough!" I thought, Kris, *what the heck are you doing?*

He turned his gaze to me, penetrating my heart with eyes full of rage. Dee, still trying to break free from his grip, shouted, "That's my dad!"

He dropped her in the sand, grabbed me by my tank-top shirt, lifted me off the ground, and started shaking me like a rag doll, yelling, "I am taking her with me! I love her! I'm taking her with me!"

I actually thought about telling him that I knew from personal experience that it wouldn't take much time living with Dee before he would bring her back. But the last ounce of strength drained from my body and the voice in my spirit grew louder and more intense: "TELL HIM ABOUT ME! TELL HIM ABOUT ME!"

Crowds of people were gathering around us and the folks who were watching the bodybuilding contest were now poised to watch a fight instead.

"I love her. I love her. I am taking her with me," he continued. But then suddenly something happened. His face changed, almost like someone struck him in the head. He looked at me and said, "What are you doing here?"

"I am a yo–yout–youth pa–pas–pastor," I stuttered.

He dropped me in the sand, stepped back a few feet, and looking stunned repeated, "A youth...youth... pas–pas–pastor?"

"TELL HIM ABOUT ME!" the voice yelled. Just then, still on my knees, I looked up and saw something

Tell him

about me.

> *My body took off after him as if it was possessed by God Himself.*
>
> ∽

like a TV screen hovering over his head. Pictures of his life began to appear on the screen. "Just tell him what you see," the Lord insisted. I saw the young man at a funeral.

On the screen above his head I saw the young man at a funeral, so I said, "Your father died last year, didn't he? And you blame yourself for his death, don't you?"

"Yes. Yes, that is true," he said through tears.

The pictured changed and I saw an old woman lying in a hospital bed with this motorcycle guy standing by her bed. "Your mother's in the hospital, isn't she? And you blame yourself for her sickness, don't you?"

"Yes, oh my God...you're right," he wailed.

The scene changed again...I saw a young boy about eight years old, going forward to receive Jesus in a little, white, country church with a steeple. "You asked Jesus into your life when you were eight years old, didn't you?"

Crying uncontrollably he blurted out, "YES! YES I DID!"

Boldness began to rise in my soul. I jumped to my feet and ran over to him. He was already kneeling in the sand, crying.

I got a few inches from his face and yelled, "You need Jesus!"

"I know!" he yelled back. (I had no idea why we were yelling in each other's ears.)

"Pray this prayer with me," I yelled. "Jesus, I need You in my life," I began.

"Jesus, I need You in my life," he repeated, yelling with me. But then he seemed to panic. He jumped to his feet and took off running wildly, stepping on people as he made his getaway. My body took off after him as if it was possessed by God Himself.

"Go after him!" the Lord insisted.

"No way!" I objected. But against my will, my body took off after him as if it was possessed by God Himself. As I was chasing the guy I thought, *What am I going to do when I catch him?* I caught up to him and jumped on his back. Both of us fell to the ground and struggled to our knees. I put my arm around his neck and yelled, "You need Jesus!"

"I know…I know," he said through his tears.

"Pray this prayer!" I shouted. "Jesus, forgive me for my sins."

He began to repeat, "Jesus, forgive me," but then he shook himself loose from me and took off running again.

Again, Jesus said, "Go after him," and again my body obeyed, ignoring my protests, and took off after him! People rushed out of the way as I tackled him again.

"You need the Lord in your life!" I shouted in his ear.

"I do. I know I do," he cried.

"Come on, pray with me. Jesus, I want to start over. I need a new start. I new a new life."

He began to repeat it, but then jumped to his feet, the war raging in his soul. He ran toward the water, wailing loudly like a son who had lost his father.

I pursued him again, falling on him at the water's edge. He repeated part of a prayer again but the battle for this man's life was too intense. He threw me off of him and ran about a hundred

> *An open vision is a picture the Lord gives you that you see with your natural eyes.*

yards down the beach, then stopped and turned around. He yelled, "Hey you!"

I struggled to my feet, and we stood like two gunfighters at a showdown.

"Yeah?" I shouted.

"You pray for me," he insisted.

"What is your name?"

He pushed back his coat and lifted up his shirt, exposing a belt buckle with his name on it in large letters.

"My name is Philip," he proclaimed.

"I will pray for you. I will!" I agreed.

Then it was over. Hundreds of people had been looking on as two men encountered their God—one man struggling for life and the other man trying to hold on to him, struggling to pull him free from the grip of utter darkness.

This was my first experience with an open vision. An open vision is a picture the Lord gives you that you see with your natural eyes. Although open visions have been rare in my own life, open visions are a dynamic way we can hear from God. This open vision sure got Philip's attention. An open vision is a picture the Lord gives you that you see with your natural eyes.

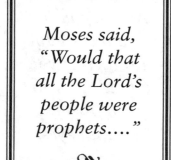

> Moses said, "Would that all the Lord's people were prophets...."

MY SHEEP HEAR MY VOICE

Let's explore some other ways God speaks to us and investigate some of the reasons we don't hear from Him more often. Many Christians don't think God speaks to them, or at least that He doesn't talk to them very often. But this isn't true. God loves to communicate with us even more than we want to listen.

Jesus died on the Cross not just to forgive our sins but ultimately to bring us into a relationship with God. Communication is probably the single greatest vehicle of any relationship. Although some people have a problem believing that God wants to talk to everybody, most believers understand that true prayer is not just throwing up a list of requests to Heaven. Prayer is personal, reciprocal communication with the Lord.

Jesus said, *"My sheep hear My voice"* (John 10:27). Prophecy, in its simplest form, is merely hearing from the Holy Spirit and repeating what He said. While few believers are called to the office of the prophet, all of God's people are called to be prophetic. The office of the prophet is specifically ordained by God to equip the saints to be prophetic—to administer that particular aspect of the grace of God that is the inheritance of every believer.

Moses said, *"Would that all the Lord's people were prophets, that the Lord would put His Spirit upon them!"* (Num. 11:29). Moses recognized the desire of the Lord for all His covenant people to hear His voice and partner with the Holy Spirit in carrying out God's purposes through prophecy. Through Christ, this desire was fulfilled as God made a new covenant with us in which, as Jeremiah prophe-

God is multilingual.

sied, His law is written on our hearts and we all know Him personally, from the least to the greatest (see Jer. 31:33-34). Moses said, "Would that all the Lord's people were prophets...."

We have trained people in prophetic ministry for more than 20 years. Thousands of people from every walk of life and denominational background have gone through our training to learn how to hear the voice of God. The feedback I get most often from the people we train is, "I have heard the voice of the Spirit most of my Christian life but I didn't know it was God."

God is multilingual. He speaks several languages. We will explore some of the ways God speaks to us in the following chapter. But the goal of this book isn't to investigate ALL the languages of the Spirit—it would take an entire volume of books just to scratch the surface of the subject—but it is for us to understand that the Lord is always speaking to us. It is our job to learn His language and understand His heart. God is multilingual.

GOD HIDES HIS WORD FOR US

Before we get into some of the languages of the Spirit, let's first look at the nature of God's communication. Luke recorded a comment of Christ's that gives some insight into this:

> *At that very time He rejoiced greatly in the Holy Spirit, and said, "I praise You, O Father, Lord of heaven and earth, that You have hidden these things from the wise and intelligent and have revealed them to infants. Yes, Father, for this way was well-pleasing in Your sight"* (Luke 10:21).

Knowledge is power and God doesn't want the prideful to be the powerful. Therefore God hides His Word so that only the hungry and the humble can find it! Did you get that? God actually hides His word and looks for His people to find it. The parables of Jesus are one of the best examples in Scripture of how the Lord conceals His treasures from the arrogant and the proud. Many have been taught that Jesus told parables to demonstrate spiritual principles with natural illustrations. However, Jesus made it clear that He told parables so that people would *not* understand truth and become powerful. Parables were told not to *reveal*

> *Knowledge is power and God doesn't want the prideful to be the powerful.*

truth, but to *hide* it. Matthew's account of the parables makes this very plain: Knowledge is power and God doesn't want the prideful to be the powerful.

> *The disciples came and said to* [Jesus], *"Why do You speak to them in parables?" Jesus answered them, "To you it has been granted to know the mysteries of the kingdom of heaven, but to them it has not been granted. For whoever has, to him more shall be given, and he will have an abundance; but whoever does not have, even what he has shall be taken away from him. Therefore I speak to them in parables; because while seeing they do not see, and while hearing they do not hear, nor do they understand....But blessed are your eyes, because they see; and your ears, because they hear"* (Matthew 13:10-13,16).

Preceding this teaching, Jesus had told the story of a man sowing seed into different types of soil. When the story ended, His message was over. No explanation was given. His disciples were the only ones who received the interpretation of the parables. So why share the story at all if He didn't want people to understand it? This question has deep roots into the heart of the King and once you understand the answer to this question, you will receive the key to the mysteries of the Kingdom of God. Parables were told not to *reveal* truth, but to *hide* it.

Parables were told not to reveal truth, but to hide it.

This key to one of the greatest mysteries of all time comes from none other than Solomon himself, who stands among the wisest men ever to have graced this planet. He said, *"It is the glory of God to conceal a matter, but the glory of kings is to search out a matter"* (Prov. 25:2). Okay, what is the great mystery of the

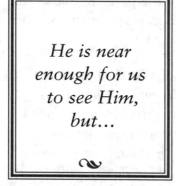

He is near enough for us to see Him, but...

ages? As Bill Johnson says, "God hides the mysteries of the Kingdom *for* us, not *from* us, because hiding them is what draws out the glory of our identity as His royal sons and daughters." When Jesus spoke in parables, He was not only preventing the hard-hearted from being responsible for revelation they weren't prepared to handle, He was creating divine opportunities for those who would believe to mature into the *kings* that God could entrust with His revelation. There is something about seeking God with all of our hearts that forms the royal character that can handle the weightiness of God's truth.

When Jesus told the parable of the sower and the seed, many people probably thought, "Why is a carpenter trying to tell farmers how to plant seed? Those carpenters think they know everything." But the men and women who were hungry and humble had a different experience. Their hearts would recognize, "I don't think He was talking about seed. I have the impression that this has something to do with the word of God and the condition of our hearts." If we are hungry for a relationship with our Creator and we have humble hearts, we will hear things no one else hears and see things no one has ever seen before. He is near enough for us to see Him, but...

DON'T LET HIM PASS YOU BY

Many people are waiting for God to come into their lives and yet they are unaware that He is passing right by them. He is near enough for us to see Him, but far enough away that it is hard for us to recognize Him. Check out the experience His disciples had:

> *When it was evening, the boat was in the middle of the sea, and He was alone on the land. Seeing them straining at the oars, for the wind was against them, at about the*

fourth watch of the night He came to them, walking on the sea; and He intended to pass by them. But when they saw Him walking on the sea, they supposed that it was a ghost, and cried out; for they all saw Him and were terrified. But immediately He spoke with them and said to them, "Take courage; it is I, do not be afraid" (Mark 6:47-50).

It is important to note here that the guys who hung out with Jesus every day didn't recognize Him walking on the water. Not only did He not look familiar to them, He seemed scary. Oftentimes the Lord will appear to us in a way that forces us to push past our fear in order to embrace Him. As I mentioned earlier, the Holy Spirit, whom He has sent to lead us into ALL truth, is appropriately called the Comforter. If we want to live a supernatural life we will need a comforter, because the "dogs of doom" are often guarding the greatest treasure of Heaven.

Another revealing fact about the nature of God is that Jesus intended to pass His disciples by—His best friends, who were straining at the oars. This experience teaches us that God is not impressed by our labors. He doesn't respond to our hard work but He loves to be with people who call out to Him and make time for Him. God is not impressed by our labors.

It is also worth noting that sometimes the ways in which the Lord comes to us make Him hard to recognize. The Book of Luke gives us another example of this:

While they were talking and discussing, Jesus Himself approached and began traveling with them. But their eyes were prevented from recognizing Him. And He said to them, "What are these words that you are exchanging with one another as you are walking?" And they stood still, looking sad. One of them,

God is not impressed by our labors.

named Cleopas, answered and said to Him, "Are You the only one visiting Jerusalem and unaware of the things which have happened here in these days?" And He said to them, "What things?" And they said to Him, "The things about Jesus the Nazarene, who was a prophet mighty in deed and word in the sight of God and all the people, and how the chief priests and our rulers delivered Him to the sentence of death, and crucified Him. But we were hoping that it was He who was going to redeem Israel. Indeed, besides all this, it is the third day since these things happened. But also some women among us amazed us. When they were at the tomb early in the morning, and did not find His body, they came, saying that they had also seen a vision of angels who said that He was alive. Some of those who were with us went to the tomb and found it just exactly as the women also had said; but Him they did not see." And He said to them, "O foolish men and slow of heart to believe in all that the prophets have spoken! Was it not necessary for the Christ to suffer these things and to enter into His glory?" Then beginning with Moses and with all the prophets, He explained to them the things concerning Himself in all the Scriptures. And they approached the village where they were going, and He acted as though He were going farther. But they urged Him, saying, "Stay with us, for it is getting toward evening, and the day is now nearly over." So He went in to stay with them. When He had reclined at the table with them, He took the bread and blessed it, and breaking it, He began giving it to them. Then their eyes were opened and they recognized Him; and He vanished from their sight. They said to one another, "Were not our hearts burning within us while He was

> How many times have we totally missed Him?

154

speaking to us on the road, while He was explaining the Scriptures to us?" (Luke 24:15-32)

These two men were experiencing God with their hearts, but they didn't discern that it was the Lord who was causing this fire in their souls until they invited Him to have dinner with them. Did you notice that Jesus intended to go on without revealing Himself to them again? Mark 16:12 says the reason they didn't recognize Him is that He came to them in a *"different form."* How many times has God come to us in a form we were not familiar with and we totally missed Him? I wonder how often we are praying for an encounter and it is sitting right next to us! How many times have we totally missed Him?

ATTITUDE IS EVERYTHING

I have learned something powerful in my experience with God. Although He doesn't always respond to our works, He does respond to a great attitude. A Canaanite woman had an experience with Jesus that shows us God will often offend our minds to reveal our heart, but He can't resist a great attitude! This story will blow your mind. Jesus called the woman "a dog," but she refused to be offended and left with her daughter delivered:

> *But she came and began to bow down before Him, saying, "Lord, help me!" And He answered and said, "It is not good to take the children's bread and throw it to the dogs." But she said, "Yes, Lord; but even the dogs feed on the crumbs which fall from their masters' table." Then Jesus said to her, "O woman, your faith is great; it shall be done for you as you wish." And her daughter was healed at once* (Matthew 15:25-28).

God responds to a great attitude.

The secret to amazing encounters with God is simple. Be humble (teachable, correctable, impressible, and moldable), stay hungry (willing to go out of your way to meet Him, to take a step beyond convenience), be unoffendable, and never let fear tell you what to do. God responds to a great attitude.

God is always speaking.

GOD'S FIRST LANGUAGE IS NOT ENGLISH

Remember, the Lord is more determined and excited to speak to us than we are to hear from Him. In fact, God is *always* speaking, but He is *not human* and His first language is *not English!* I don't mean that God can't speak in a human language. I am simply saying that there are languages that are common to the spirit world but are not perceivable in the natural realm at all. If the only equipment we have for listening to God is our natural ears and eyes, we will not be able to distinguish most of the activity of Heaven. God is *always* speaking.

For example, in the room we are in right now there is music playing all around us. But even if we were to close our eyes and listen carefully, we wouldn't be able to hear it. However, by simply *turning on a radio, we would be able to perceive what was there all along.* The reason, of course, is that our human bodies were never designed to perceive radio waves. Radio receivers turn radio waves into sound waves so we can perceive and understand them.

RECEIVING EQUIPMENT

If we are hungry and humble, we can ask the Lord for the gifts of the Spirit and He will give them to us. Then we will begin to see what we have never seen before and hear what was once indistinguishable—so we can do what has never been done before. The gifts of the Holy Spirit are to the spirit realm what radio and television are to the natural realm. We need this equipment to tap into Heaven's sound waves. The gifts of the Holy Spirit are to the spirit realm what radio and television are to the natural realm.

There is a great Old Testament example of a spiritually blind person getting equipped to see into the invisible realm. In Second Kings 6 we read that Elisha's prophetic anointing gave him the ability to hear what the king of Aram said in secret to his troops. Elisha became a secret weapon to the king of Israel by revealing the plans of this enemy king. Then the king of Aram decided to capture Elisha. One morning Elisha's servant discovered that the city where they were staying was completely encircled by this enemy army. In a panic, the servant ran to tell Elisha they were in trouble. But then something very powerful occurred. Elisha prayed for his servant and immediately his eyes were opened to see that the mountains were full of the horses and chariots of God. It is important to understand that the horses and chariots were already there because Elisha traveled with a heavenly entourage. The servant just couldn't see them until he received an impartation from the seer. The servant couldn't see them until he received an impartation from the seer.

This kind of prophetic gift is now available to all believers in the New Testament Church. The Bible says, *"For you can all prophesy one by one, so that all may learn and all may be exhorted"* (1 Cor. 14:31). Spiritual equipping is needed from God so we are able to perceive what is taking place in the invisible kingdoms all around us. Without these spiritual gifts we're blind people in the Kingdom of God!

> *The gifts of the Holy Spirit are to the spirit realm what radio and television are to the natural realm.*

THE POWER OF IMPARTATION

The most common way to receive spiritual gifts is by having someone who already is gifted lay hands on you and pray for the

> *The servant couldn't see them until he received an impartation from the seer.*

gift or gifts to be imparted to you. Paul wrote this to the church in Rome. *"For I long to see you so that I may impart some spiritual gift to you, that you may be established"* (Rom. 1:11). It is amazing that Paul equates "impartation" with being "established." In other words, if you haven't received spiritual impartation, you are on shaky ground in the Kingdom. In the Book of Acts we catch a glimpse of how the early Church practically received the gifts of the Spirit from spiritual fathers. Luke writes, *"When Paul had laid his hands upon them, the Holy Spirit came on them, and they began speaking with tongues and prophesying"* (Acts 19:6).

Paul exhorted his disciple, Timothy, about the stewardship of his impartation. He said:

> *Do not neglect the spiritual gift within you, which was bestowed on you through prophetic utterance with the laying on of hands by the presbytery. Take pains with these things; be absorbed in them, so that your progress will be evident to all* (1 Timothy 4:14-15).

Notice how Paul teaches Timothy that he needs to take responsibility for what has been imparted to him by *taking pains* with it. The word "pains" here means "intense labor." We must work with the gifts in a way that the people around us can see our progress.

The impartation of spiritual gifts through the laying on of hands is considered to be one of the elementary teachings of Christ, and is actually a principle found in the very roots of Jewish culture. It was the reason Jacob was blessed and Esau was cursed. Hebrews includes this principle with the other elementary principles of the faith:

> *Therefore leaving the elementary teaching about the Christ, let us press on to maturity, not laying again a foundation of repentance from dead works and of faith toward God, of instruction about washings and **laying on of hands**, and the resurrection of the dead and eternal judgment* (Hebrews 6:1-2).

The gifts of the Spirit are not awards, something we earn by our great behavior or performance. They are gifts, something we received for free. The word "gifts" comes from the Greek word *charisma*, which means "a divine enablement granted as a favor." We can't do anything to earn God's gifts but we are commanded to *"desire earnestly spiritual **gifts**, but especially that you may prophesy"* (1 Cor. 14:1). Some people treat the gifts of the Spirit as an option. I really don't understand that attitude at all. God told us to ask for them and desire them. The gifts of the Spirit are not awards.

The gifts of the Spirit are not awards.

BELIEVING IS DOING SIGNS AND WONDERS

Jesus was very bold about signs and wonders following us. He said:

> *He who has believed and has been baptized shall be saved; but he who has disbelieved shall be condemned. These signs will accompany those who have believed: in My name they will cast out demons, they will speak with new tongues; they will pick up serpents, and if they drink any deadly poison, it will not hurt them; they will lay hands on the sick, and they will recover* (Mark 16:16-18).

Preceding this statement Jesus declared, *"He who has believed and has been baptized shall be saved; but he who has disbelieved shall be condemned"* (Mark 16:16). Then He defined what it meant to believe. We simply can't afford to miss what's at stake

> *The urgency to develop a supernatural lifestyle is non-negotiable.*
>
> ❧

in learning to walk by the faith that leaves a wake of signs and wonders behind it.

It is also important to note that He didn't say, "These signs will follow the leaders who believe" or "These signs will follow certain special people who believe." Neither did He say, "These signs will follow the first-century disciples who believe." Jesus said, "These signs will follow *those* who believe!" If you call yourself a believer in Jesus Christ, the urgency to develop a supernatural lifestyle is non-negotiable for your life. The urgency to develop a supernatural lifestyle is non-negotiable.

I was ministering at a ministry school some time ago. I read Mark 16 to the students and then yelled, "Jesus said these signs will follow those who believe. Is there enough evidence in your life to convict you in the courts of Heaven of being a Christian?" I know it sounds a little harsh, but it is a great, and in fact, an essential question. Leaders who teach a powerless gospel or who tolerate a gift-less church lack theological integrity. Is there enough evidence to convict you in the courts of Heaven?

WARNINGS

> *Is there enough evidence to convict you in the courts of Heaven?*
>
> ❧

The gifts of the Spirit, unlike the fruit of the Spirit, are not marks of our maturity in God, because we receive them simply by impartation. The truth is that sometimes the most spiritually gifted people have the worst character. It is so important for us to realize that the fact that just because someone can heal the sick or cast out demons *doesn't mean* they are great leaders or that their doctrine is accurate. Walking in power never takes the place of great character. But neither does great character excuse us from demonstrating our faith through the signs that Jesus insisted on when He said, "*These signs will follow those who believe.*" Walking in power never takes the place of great character.

> *Walking in power never takes the place of great character.*

Jesus made another statement that is so challenging that if you catch the revelation, it will alter the way you live your life forever. He proclaimed, "*Truly, truly, I say to you, he who believes in Me, the works that I do, he will do also; and greater works than these he will do; because I go to the Father*" (John 14:12). You will do greater works than Jesus if you believe in Him. Now that's amazing! The Greek word "greater" is the word *megas*, which is where we get our prefix "mega." *Megas* means exceedingly, greatest, large, loud, strong, and mighty. We are called to do **mega-works** with God—to do Mission Impossible! That's the Great Commission.

CHAPTER 9

Learning Foreign Languages

In the last chapter, we learned the importance of receiving a spiritual radio so that we can pick up the voice of the Lord. As an interesting side note, the Greek word for "voice" is the word *phone*. I like to think that God wants us to develop our spiritual receivers so He can install His presidential phone in His holy temple (us). We all need eyes to see and ears to hear what the Spirit is saying to His people.

In this chapter we will explore some of the languages of the Spirit. Earlier I said that God isn't human and His first language isn't English—or Spanish, French, Italian, or any other human language, for that matter. What is the language of Heaven, then? Let's look into the Bible and see if we can discover the answer to this question.

The Book of Acts is an excellent place for us to begin our investigation. Peter, quoting the Book of Joel, declared that in the last Days, people would hear God through visions, dreams, and prophecy:

The Holy Spirit draws on the blackboard of our imagination.

"And it shall be in the last days," God says, *"that I will pour forth of my spirit on all mankind; and your sons and your daughters shall prophesy, and your young men shall see visions, and your old men shall dream dreams; even on my bondslaves, both men and women, I will in those days pour forth of my spirit and they shall prophesy"* (Acts 2:17-18).

By declaring that Pentecost was a fulfillment of Joel's prophecy, Peter was officially stating that the Last Days had begun. Therefore we are in the Last Days and these promises are as true for us as for these first-century believers. This passage implies that the language of dreams, visions, and prophecy by which He will speak to His people will bridge generational barriers, crash through the gender gap, and cross all social boundaries. Christians from all walks of life should be able to live in the Spirit and learn how to hear the voice of God.

Visions, dreams, and prophecy are not the only ways the Holy Spirit speaks to us but they are the most common sources of communication. Let's explore visions and dreams.

VISIONS OF THE MIND

There are two types of visions. One is a *vision of the mind*, in which the Lord "projects" images and pictures onto the "screen" of our minds. This could also be called a "sanctified imagination," or an imagination that is under the influence of the Holy Spirit. This is one of the most common ways the Holy Spirit speaks to us. The Holy Spirit draws on the blackboard of our imagination.

I like to explain this by having people picture a pink elephant in their minds. No one has ever seen a pink elephant before because they don't exist. But we are able to envision something with our minds that our eyes have never witnessed. The ability to form pictures in our minds is one of the vehicles the Spirit uses to communicate with us. The Holy Spirit draws pictures or projects images on this blackboard of our imagination.

When God speaks to us through visions of the mind, it is easy to miss the "you've got mail" message, first, because it feels like our own thoughts or imagination, and second, because these types of visions often only last a split second—they come and go in a flash. But the more we understand God's intention to speak through our minds, the more we can anticipate and recognize it when He does.

> *Virtual reality dreams, or visions of the night, are to your spirit what movies are to your natural man.*

OPEN VISIONS

The second kind of vision is called an *open vision*. This is an image that you are seeing with your *natural* eyes. I gave you an example of an open vision in the story of the motor-cycle guy on the beach in the previous chapter. Open visions are not as common as visions of the mind but are a very powerful way to receive revelation. When you have an open vision you are still aware of the world around you. You can usually interact with people while you are experiencing the vision. It is actually very much like watching television—think of it as Holy Ghost TV.

DREAMS

Dreams are another primary language of the Holy Spirit. There are two types of dreams. One is what I call *virtual reality dreams*. This kind of dream is actually a vision of the mind that we have while we sleep and remember when we wake up. Virtual reality dreams, or visions of the night, are to your spirit what movies are to your natural man. Virtual reality dreams, or visions of the night, are to your spirit what movies are to your natural man.

Here is an example of a virtual reality dream that Nebuchadnezzar had in the days of Daniel. We know it was this type of dream because it was symbolic and needed an interpretation:

> *You, O king, were looking and behold, there was a single great statue; that statue, which was large and of extraordinary splendor, was standing in front of you, and its appearance was awesome. The head of that statue was made of fine gold, its breast and its arms of silver, its belly and its thighs of bronze, its legs of iron, its feet partly of iron and partly of clay. You continued looking until a stone was cut out without hands, and it struck the statue on its feet of iron and clay and crushed them. Then the iron, the clay, the bronze, the silver and the gold were crushed all at the same time and became like chaff from the summer threshing floors; and the wind carried them away so that not a trace of them was found. But the stone that struck the statue became a great mountain and filled the whole earth. This was the dream; now we will tell its*
>
> *interpretation before the king* (Daniel 2:31-36).

> *A reality dream is a real experience that our spirit has with the spirit world while our soul is sleeping.*

The second type of dream I call a *reality dream*. This is a *real experience* that our spirit has with the spirit world while our soul is sleeping. There is no day or night in the spirit world. Our spirit is always awake and sometimes we remember an experience our inner man had as we slept. If you have ever awakened from a full night's sleep feeling tired because it felt like you were in a war all night, you probably were! A *reality dream* is a *real experience* that our spirit has with the spirit world while our soul is sleeping.

A great example of this type of dream is found in Genesis 20:

Abraham said of Sarah his wife, "She is my sister." So Abimelech king of Gerar sent and took Sarah. But God came to Abimelech in a dream of the night, and said to him, "Behold, you are a dead man because of the woman whom you have taken, for she is married." Now Abimelech had not come near her; and he said, "Lord, will You slay a nation, even though blameless? Did he not himself say to me, 'She is my sister'? And she herself said, 'He is my brother.' In the integrity of my heart and the innocence of my hands I have done this." Then God said to him in the dream, "Yes, I know that in the integrity of your heart you have done this, and I also kept you from sinning against Me; therefore I did not let you touch her" (Genesis 20:2-6).

Notice it *doesn't* say that *Abimelech dreamt* of God but it describes a *real encounter Abimelech had with the Lord* that he remembered when he woke up. I'm convinced that these spiritual night adventures are more common than most people think they are.

Another example of a *reality dream* is in the well-known story of Joseph in Matthew 2. In this event, an angel of the Lord interacted with Joseph while he slept:

Now when they had gone, behold, an angel of the Lord appeared to Joseph in a dream and said, "Get up! Take the Child and His mother and flee to Egypt, and remain there until I tell you; for Herod is going to search for the Child to destroy Him." So Joseph got up and took the Child and His mother while it was still night, and left for Egypt (Matthew 2:13-14).

JOB'S INSIGHTS INTO DREAMS

There is much to know about the mysterious world of dreams. Job gives us some insight into the nature of dreams and their purposes:

Indeed God speaks once, or twice, yet no one notices it. In a dream, a vision of the night, when sound sleep falls on men, while they slumber in their beds, then He opens the ears of men, and seals their instruction, that He may turn man aside from his conduct, and keep man from pride; He keeps back his soul from the pit, and his life from passing over into Sheol (Job 33:14-18).

Job says that the dreams of God often go unnoticed. It seems strange that the God of the universe can be speaking to us and we don't even know it. You would think that any experience with God would be a memorable one, but it deserves repeating that God loves to *hide* His word for us. Job says that the dreams of God often go unnoticed.

Job also reinforces the fact that virtual reality dreams are visions of the night. He goes on to explain that many times God

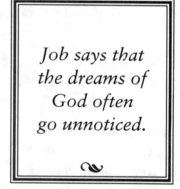

Job says that the dreams of God often go unnoticed.

uses dreams to change our attitude. If our soul is resisting the Lord, He waits until we are unconscious and then changes our heart through visions of the night. He even says that these midnight encounters can keep us from hell!

A friend of ours told us how his son's marriage was restored by a dream! His son and daughter-in-law were in a year-long, ugly custody battle over their only son. Their marriage was over and although the husband had had a change of heart and wanted to reconcile with his wife, she remained hurt, angry, and bitter. She refused any counsel. She broke all ties with the family and would have nothing to do with any of them.

The night before they were to go to divorce court, his daughter-in-law had a dream. In it she saw herself standing at the edge of a beautiful meadow. Her husband was standing in the middle of the field, and suddenly Jesus appeared in the field. He looked over at her, smiled, and then walked through the meadow to her husband and gave him a hug. The scene changed. Her father-in-law was now standing in the center of the field and again the Lord appeared. He looked over at her a second time and smiled while He embraced her father-in-law. In the next scene, she saw herself standing in the field of flowers. Jesus appeared off in the distance walking through the meadow towards her. Just as the Lord reached out to embrace her, she woke up. She knew the Lord was giving her the grace she needed to restore her relationship with her husband. She got out of bed at five o'clock in the morning and called her husband. They reconciled that very day and lived happily ever after!

Dreams are an amazing way to hear God. There are some important things to remember about dreams.

Not all dreams are from God.

- ✧ Not all dreams are from God. We can hear from three sources in the spirit realm—our spirit, the Holy Spirit, and evil spirits—and this is true even in our dreams. Not all dreams are from God.

- ✧ It does not necessarily mean we are prophetic just because we have dreams. Remember, even wicked people in the Old Testament had dreams. *Interpreting* dreams is what makes us prophetic.

- ✧ Colors, numbers, and other symbolic occurrences in dreams are very important to the interpretation of the dream. But even as we learn to recognize consistencies in this symbolic language, we need to remember that ultimately the interpretation of dreams belongs to the Lord.

- ✧ If we want to have more dreams, we need to become good stewards of revelations we receive. It is a great idea to put a notebook or recorder by your bed before you go to sleep.

Pray and tell the Lord, "Your servant is listening." As soon as you have a dream, write it down or record all of the details you can remember, including the way you felt about the dream while you were having it. To have more dreams, become good stewards of the revelations received.

There is so much more to know about dreams and visions. John Paul Jackson, James and Michal Ann Goll, and Cindy Jacobs have all written amazing books on the subject with deep insights into this language of God. I highly recommend their books.

WORDS OF KNOWLEDGE

The Holy Spirit will often talk to us through the avenue the Bible calls *a word of knowledge.* Paul writes, *"For to one is given the word of wisdom through the Spirit, and to another **the word of knowledge** according to the same Spirit"* (1 Cor. 12:8). A word of knowledge, unlike prophecy, is a fact or facts communicated to us by the Lord. People often confuse prophecy with the word of knowledge. Prophecy is about the future, something that has yet to occur. Many times when we speak to people by the Spirit about their life, it turns out to be something they already do. As an example, let's say you share with someone a word like, "I see you as a nurse," and the person is already a nurse. This is a word of knowledge, not a prophecy. A word of knowledge can be about any subject and it can come to us through different avenues and venues but it is always about a present reality. A word of knowledge is a fact or facts communicated to us by the Lord.

> *To have more dreams, become good stewards of the revelations received.*
>
> ❧

RECEIVING WORDS OF KNOWLEDGE THROUGH DREAMS AND VISIONS

Dreams and visions are one of the ways we can receive words of knowledge.

Many years ago I had a powerful experience in a dream that contained a word of knowledge.

While we lived in Weaverville, Kathy and I owned an auto parts store that grew very quickly. Several of our wholesale customers began to stock our products and we needed to have more price levels to facilitate them. We reached a point where our store's computer system

> *A word of knowledge is a fact or facts communicated to us by the Lord.*
>
> relax

desperately needed to be upgraded to accommodate our growing customer base, but we didn't have the money to do it.

I talked to the programmer who wrote the software and explained my dilemma to him. He tried for a week to expand the software from three to five price levels. But he finally called and told me the software was simply not designed to do what we needed it to do. He recommended we replace the program with a more powerful system. I had another computer tech come up from Redding to try to fix it but after a couple of days, he came to the same conclusion.

I am, personally, computer illiterate. I don't know much more than how to turn the dang things on. But one night, I went to sleep and I had a dream. In the dream, I clearly saw a sequence of numbers, letters, and symbols in a particular order. I woke up with them burned into my mind, like an imprinted image that remains when you stare into a light. I got up quickly and wrote it all down.

At three o'clock in the morning I woke Kathy up and explained to her what had happened. She was in no mood for my "revelation" and tried to go back to sleep. But I was too excited to let her sleep and finally convinced her to get up and go to the parts house with me.

She was pretty uptight with me because she wasn't a believer yet—she believed in Jesus; it was *me* she was having a hard time with. We finally arrived at the parts house at about 4:00 A.M. My wife turned the computer on and typed the first sequence of numbers in, and suddenly the screen changed.

Kathy looked stunned. She said, "I think it just took us to the back of the program!" I didn't even know there was a "back of the program" but I was just excited that it did something.

"Give me the rest of those numbers," she said, the frustration in her voice diminishing. She put them in and the page changed again. "I think something happened," she said with excitement. She was starting to be convinced. We went to the customer screen, and lo and behold, there were five price levels there! We used that system for several more years. Now that is a word of knowledge!

BODY CHECKS

Another way the Lord speaks to us is through a type of word of knowledge we call *body checks*. Most often the Holy Spirit uses body checks to communicate His desire to heal someone else's body. He does this by causing pain or a sensation in a certain part of the prophetic person's body that correlates to the sickness in a person who needs to be healed. (If you receive this kind of information from the Holy Spirit, it is important that you are aware of pain or discomfort that is common to you. You don't want to get your pain confused with the Lord's word of knowledge.) We see hundreds of people healed this way every month. I think most believers often miss this type of word of knowledge.

TRANCES

Trances are another way the Spirit communicates to His people. The Greek word for *trance* means "to be out of your mind." When someone is in a trance, he or she is literally out of their mind and engulfed in the mind of Christ. A person who is in a trance is completely unaware of their surroundings. You can pick them up and move them without disturbing them. In a trance, a person is literally out of their mind and engulfed in the mind of Christ.

Trances were common in the early Church. The Book of Acts records that both Peter and Paul experienced trances. Here is Luke's account of Peter's trance:

> *On the next day, as they were on their way and approaching the city, Peter went up on the housetop about the sixth hour to pray. But he became hungry and was desiring to eat; but while they were making preparations, he fell into a trance; and he saw the sky opened up, and an object like a great sheet coming down, lowered by four corners to the ground, and there were in it all kinds of four-footed animals and crawling creatures of the earth and birds of the air. A voice came to him, "Get up, Peter, kill and eat!" But Peter said, "By no means, Lord, for I have never eaten anything unholy and unclean." Again a voice came to him a second time, "What God has cleansed, no longer consider unholy." This happened three times, and immediately the object was taken up into the sky. Now while Peter was greatly perplexed in mind as to what the vision which he had seen might be, behold, the men who had been sent by Cornelius, having asked directions for Simon's house, appeared at the gate* (Acts 10:9-17).

> *In a trance, a person is literally out of their mind and engulfed in the mind of Christ.*

Peter calls his experience a *trance* and later says he was perplexed about the *vision* he had seen. When people are in trances, they often see or even interact with a vision, much like a virtual reality dream. Trances are sovereign acts of the Holy Spirit. They are not something we try to create, like a hypnotist does.

I have seen many people in trances over the years. I have carried several people, including little children, to the car while they were in a trance. Some trances last more than 12 hours. I have witnessed God changing people's hearts more times in trances than almost any other way. Even Peter's heart change towards the Gentiles began with a trance.

EXPERIENCING TRANCES

One of the most powerful experiences I ever witnessed happened to a lady in a trance. A while back, I ministered at Family Christian Center in Orangeville, California. Afterwards, as I exited the sanctuary, I met a couple at the door. We were making small talk and they were thanking me for my ministry. Suddenly the Lord spoke to me: "Ask her if she wants to see the two children she miscarried."

I was stunned. I didn't have a clue what the Lord meant by this. I also didn't know these folks, so I was unaware if they really ever had had miscarriages. I decided to ask them how many children they had. The lady told me they had two daughters.

"Have you ever had a miscarriage?" I pressed.

Her husband, looking quite defensive, said, "Yes, my wife has had two miscarriages."

By now his wife was choking back tears and I could see just bringing up the subject was really painful.

"Would you like to go see them?" I asked the woman.

"What do you mean by that?" they asked in unison.

"I don't know. The Lord just told me to ask you if you wanted to see your children."

"Yes! Oh yes, I would! I very much would!" the woman shouted.

I laid my hands on her to pray, not knowing what was going to happen. Instantly she fell into a trance. She interacted with her two children, who were in Heaven, for about an hour while we looked on. When it was over she was glowing. She said the most amazing peace came over her and all of her grief vanished. What a wonderful God we have. He knows how to take care of the deepest hurts and heal the most broken people.

I have personally seen many people visit Heaven in trances—all with the same wonderful results.

DISCERNMENT

The gift of discernment or the "distinguishing of spirits" as the Bible calls it, is probably one of the most powerful and yet misunderstood tools in a Christian's arsenal. Paul wrote to the Corinthians about this gift. He said that the Holy Spirit gives different gifts to people, *"to another the effecting of miracles, and to another prophecy, and to another **the distinguishing of spirits**, to another various kinds of tongues, and to another the interpretation of tongues"* (1 Cor. 12:10). Many prophetic people experience discernment without even realizing it. Discernment is the ability to know the source of the spiritual activity.

Discernment is the ability to know the source of the spiritual activity that is working in or through people and/or organizations. The gift of discernment can also be used to sense the compelling spirits that rule geographic areas.

The Holy Spirit communicates discernment in different ways to us. Most people who have this gift sense evil spirits by "feeling" or "hearing" them. For example, if a spirit of fear is oppressing a person in a geographic area close to you, you might suddenly feel fearful as well. If a person who walks by

> *Discernment is the ability to know the source of the spiritual activity.*

> *Many people are misdiagnosed as bipolar when they are actually experiencing the gift of discernment.*

you in a supermarket has a spirit of depression on them, you may feel depressed when you encounter them.

Years ago I was one of our main counselors at Bethel Church. When people came into my office for counseling, I would lay my hands on them and pray for them before I would let them tell me about their situation. I was using my gift of discernment to help decide where their bondage was rooted. If an evil spirit was a part of their problem, the spirit would trouble me when I touched them. For instance, if they had a problem with pornography, when I laid my hands on them I would have illicit pictures or thoughts come to my mind, usually followed by the same inappropriate feelings.

On the other hand, if they had a personal struggle with pornography and I wasn't troubled by that spirit when I touched them, I knew their problem was strictly rooted in their humanity and evil spirits weren't a factor. Discernment is very helpful in setting people free from their destructive patterns and behaviors. Many people are misdiagnosed as bipolar when they are actually experiencing the gift of discernment.

If a believer doesn't realize how the gift of discernment operates in them, it can drive them crazy! I believe many people are often misdiagnosed as bipolar when they are actually experiencing the gift of discernment, but have not been trained to use their equipment. Discerning spirits without an understanding of the gift can cause severe mood swings.

AVOIDING FRIENDLY FIRE

The Lord didn't give us the gift of discernment just to detect evil spirits. When we operate in this gift we can also determine if the Holy Spirit, the human spirit, or angels are causing a certain manifestation or attitude. Anyone who thinks they can discern the spiritual source of someone's outward manifestation simply through observation is greatly mistaken and very inexperienced in the things of the Spirit. Just think of some of the experiences people had in the Bible. Here is what Daniel wrote after one of his long encounters with God:

> *Then I, Daniel, was exhausted and sick for days. Then I got up again and carried on the king's business; but I was astounded at the vision, and there was none to explain it* (Daniel 8:27).

Daniel, you talked to God and you left sick and confused? That sounds like the fruit of an evil spirit, not the Holy Spirit. But no, it was God! Remember, this is the same God who picked up Ezekiel by the hair and suspended him in midair! I am sure most of us would initially conclude that he was under demonic attack.

The Scripture's list of odd God manifestations reads like "Ripley's Believe It or Not" TV show. I have watched people have encounters with God that I was sure were manifestations of evil spirits, but upon a later interview it was clear that they were having a Holy Spirit encounter.

A great example of this happened a few years ago. I watched a young Asian man, screaming and writhing in pain, crawl completely across our sanctuary with five people trying to cast demons out of him. A few hours later, when the manifestation finally lifted, I interviewed the man. He was quietly sobbing as he told me about his experience. He said the Lord took him in the Spirit to China and he was allowed to see all the lost souls. God allowed him to feel His heart for the lost and sense how the Lord grieves over them. When he was done sharing, I was weeping with him. We need to grow in discernment in order to value the things of the Spirit.

One more thing about discernment: Suspicion is the evil stepmother of discernment. I have watched people be assassinated and their impeccable reputations destroyed in the name of discernment. Often the witch hunters have no facts or evidence, nor can they find bad fruit in the life of the one they are accusing. Jealous and fearful people often operate out of suspicion and call it discernment. Beware! This could be you or you could be their next victim. Suspicion is the evil stepmother of discernment.

WHEN GOD WHISPERS

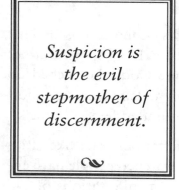

Suspicion is the evil stepmother of discernment.

It is amazing how the voice of God often comes without fanfare or drama, but instead is heard in the quiet whispers of the inner spirit. These encounters are frequently experienced as intimate moments, passing thoughts, sudden impressions, or an internal "sense" of something the Lord is saying to us. The still, small voice of God is illustrated in the Book of First Kings:

So He said, "Go forth and stand on the mountain before the Lord." And behold, the Lord was passing by! And a great and strong wind was rending the mountains and breaking in pieces the rocks before the Lord; but the Lord was not in the wind. And after the wind an earthquake, but the Lord was not in the earthquake. After the earthquake a fire, but the Lord was not in the fire; and after the fire a sound of a gentle blowing. When Elijah heard it, he wrapped his face in his mantle and went out and stood in the entrance of the cave. And behold, a voice came to him and said, "What are you doing here, Elijah?" (1 Kings 19:11-13)

This is an amazing account of God visiting His prophet in a time of distress. Although there was quite an exhibit going on around God, He was not part of any of it. Interestingly, this was the same mountain where many years before He had met the Israelites to make covenant with them, and that time, He *was* in the midst of a loud, terrifying display of power. But this time, He was not in the strong wind, nor was He present in the earthquake or the fire. He was in the gentle blowing. Elijah was a mature prophet who emerged from the cave at the sound of a quiet breeze and found His Lord there. You will, too. Quiet your soul, still your spirit, and listen—He will meet you there!

CHAPTER 10

Weapons of Mass Construction

❧

FLYING THE NOT-SO-FRIENDLY SKIES

I was flying the friendly skies one day and managed to get an upgrade to first class. As I took my seat, I noticed that the man sitting next to me seemed to be deep in thought. He was working out an algebraic equation several pages long. I leaned over and introduced myself. He, avoiding eye contact, muttered his name and continued to focus on his notes.

I said, "It looks like you're working on quite a complicated algebraic equation there, buddy. What do you do for a living?"

Still not looking up, he said, "I am an astrophysicist."

"And what does an astrophysicist do for a living?' I asked, in complete ignorance.

Rolling his eyes, he answered, "We calculate the movement of the stars and planets in the universe."

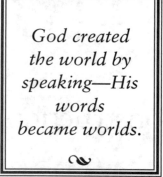

> *God created the world by speaking—His words became worlds.*

"Wow," I responded, still trying to connect. "I just read an article in a science magazine about the new telescope scientists have developed recently." (Actually one of our team members read it to us in a staff meeting. I have since asked God to forgive me for lying.) "The article stated that the telescope provided a breakthrough in astronomy that has allowed astronomers to discover that the universe is still growing."

This roused him. Looking extremely upset, he stared at me, raised his voice and proclaimed, "That is not news! What is news is that the universe is not growing proportionately, but is expanding in one direction towards something!"

I was stunned. I asked, "Does God work into this equation?"

"I don't get paid to know that!" he responded angrily.

"I do!" I fired back. "I'm a pastor."

"You talk too much!" he said, as he turned his entire body away from me. After this conversation I remembered that God worked six days and rested only on the seventh. Apparently, He must have gone back to work on the eighth day, because creation is still growing. God created the world by speaking—His words became worlds.

God created the world by speaking the elements into being. His words became worlds. I guess prophesying things into existence must be hard work if God needed to rest after six days of doing this stuff. But what's really exciting for us is that God has invited His kids to join Him in this co-creating venture through the gifts of the Spirit. Whether mountain-moving, topography-changing proclamations or prophetic declarations that transform a valley of dry bones into a field of dreams, the gifts of the Spirit are "Weapons of Mass Construction!"

PROPHECY DEFINED

Prophecy really has two dimensions, foretelling and forthtelling. Foretelling is the ability to know and declare the future. Foretelling is the most commonly understood attribute of the prophetic ministry. Foretelling is like being put into a time machine that thrusts you into the future. As foretellers, prophetic people are historians of events that have yet to happen. To be more accurate, we are able to foretell events because we are seated with Christ in heavenly places outside of time, which enables us to have a timeless perspective. The gift of the Holy Spirit and the seat of Christ cohabiting in and through us supercharge New Testament prophetic ministry, causing us to have extremely accurate information about the future. (I explain the timeless zone in more detail in my first book, *The Supernatural Ways of Royalty*.) Foretelling is like being put into a time machine that thrusts you into the future.

> *Foretelling is like being put into a time machine that thrusts you into the future.*

GRACEFUL FORTHTELLING

The second dimension of prophetic ministry is forthtelling. Forthtelling is different from foretelling. Forthtelling is the God-given ability to *cause* the future! In other words, forthtelling is co-creating with God. Forthtelling is facilitated in two ways. One way is through the grace of God, and the other way is by the ministry of the angels who are the servants of the Lord. Forthtelling is the God-given ability to cause the future!

Let's look first at forthtelling that manifests through the grace of God. A great example of this type of prophecy is captured in the Book of Ezekiel:

> *The hand of the Lord was upon me, and He brought me out by the Spirit of the Lord and set me down in the middle*

> *Forthtelling is the God-given ability to cause the future!*
>
> ❧

of the valley; and it was full of bones. He caused me to pass among them round about, and behold, there were very many on the surface of the valley; and lo, they were very dry. He said to me, "Son of man, can these bones live?" And I answered, "O Lord God, You know." Again He said to me, "Prophesy over these bones and say to them, 'O dry bones, hear the word of the Lord.' Thus says the Lord God to these bones, 'Behold, I will cause breath to enter you that you may come to life. I will put sinews on you, make flesh grow back on you, cover you with skin and put breath in you that you may come alive; and you will know that I am the Lord.'" So I prophesied as I was commanded; and as I prophesied, there was a noise, and behold, a rattling; and the bones came together, bone to its bone. And I looked, and behold, sinews were on them, and flesh grew and skin covered them; but there was no breath in them. Then He said to me, "Prophesy to the breath, prophesy, son of man, and say to the breath, 'Thus says the Lord God, "Come from the four winds, O breath, and breathe on these slain, that they come to life."'" So I prophesied as He commanded me, and the breath came into them, and they came to life and stood on their feet, an exceedingly great army* (Ezekiel 37:1-10).

A valley of dead, dry bones became an awesome army as Ezekiel prophesied to them. He wasn't just telling the future; he was creating new realities as he spoke for and with God. His words became worlds. We are commissioned to speak for God in a way that causes the invisible world to emerge and become tangible.

This whole thing became real to me in April 1995. I had just finished speaking at a conference in a church in Santa Rosa,

California. After the meeting, two of the elders, Gene and Lisa, took Kathy and me out to eat. We ordered lunch and things were going well until something crazy happened. The Lord spoke to me and said, "Tell Lisa that at this time next year she is going to have a child!"

> *"If you don't tell her, she won't get pregnant!"*
>
> ❧

Gene and Lisa had been married for more than 13 years and they had been unable to have children. They had just adopted two little boys. In fact, they were going to court the following day to complete the adoption process. I was stunned! I knew their journey so well that I had no faith for this.

"Lord, I am not going to tell her that. You tell her," I replied. "If you don't tell her, she won't get pregnant!"

Then Jesus made a statement that changed my life. He said, "IF YOU DON'T TELL HER, SHE WON'T GET PREGNANT!"

My head was spinning. How could this be true? Was I supposed to believe that my words would determine whether or not a child would come into this world?

I decided to whisper the prophecy in Lisa's ear. I was going to say, "Lisa, God says that at this time next year you are going to have a child—it may be a spiritual child." I leaned over and began to whisper the word in her ear, but before I could get out "It may be a spiritual child," Lisa began shouting, "I am going to get pregnant! I'm going to have a child!"

Gene didn't hear what I said to her, but when he heard Lisa's response he chimed in, "Wow, that's awesome!"

My wife, sitting across the table from me, was giving me a killer stare as if to say, "You stupid man. What have you done?"

It was a very long and quiet drive home. But a couple of months later, Lisa called and left a message on our answering

> *The prophet's reward is the ability to do something that couldn't be before the prophetic word was received.*

machine: "Kris, this is Lisa. I thought you might want to know that I am pregnant!"

Lisa and Gene had a beautiful child and are now pastors in Round Mountain, Nevada.

How did Lisa receive the ability to conceive? She received something the Bible calls "the prophet's reward." Jesus said, *"He who receives a prophet in the name of a prophet shall receive a prophet's reward; and he who receives a righteous man in the name of a right-eous man shall receive a righteous man's reward"* (Matt. 10:41). What is a prophet's reward? The prophet's reward is the ability to do what you couldn't do one second before you received the prophetic word. We call this God-given ability *grace*. Grace is more than undeserved favor. Grace is the operational power of God. The prophet's reward is the ability to do something that couldn't be before the prophetic word was received.

Maybe it is easier for you to picture it this way. Let's say, for the sake of discussion, that your human words are red. But when you are speaking for God, on your red words there is blue. The blue is what makes your words a prophecy. The blue is grace, the operational power of God. It is the blue that causes your words to have the transforming power of the Kingdom. It is the blue that is Heaven invading earth.

The only thing that makes a declaration a true prophecy is the blue on the red. It doesn't matter if you yell, shake, sound like Shakespeare, quote the Bible, or stand on your head—the only thing that counts is that there is blue on the red, *grace*. Grace can pull the worst sinner out of the deepest darkness; grace can transform a mass murderer into a super-apostle. Grace can alter the course of world history, raise a dead person, move a mountain, gift the giftless, change the rebellious, and restore a marriage. Grace can make sad people drunk with laughter, cause the hopeless to hope again, heal sick folks, and release the most demonized prisoner into a life of freedom. Zechariah described this kind of mountain-moving grace when he said, *"What are you, O great mountain? Before Zerubbabel you will become a plain; and he will bring forth the top stone with shouts of 'Grace, grace to it!'"* (Zech. 4:7). Grace is the prophet's reward! Prophetic declarations are the vehicles that grace rides on. Grace can transform a mass murderer into a super-apostle.

Paul talked about gift-equipping grace in the Book of Ephesians. He said:

> *But to each one of us grace was given according to the measure of Christ's gift....And He gave some as apostles, and some as prophets, and some as evangelists, and some as pastors and teachers, for the equipping of the saints for the work of service, to the building up of the body of Christ* (Ephesians 4:7,11-12).

This gift-giving grace was highlighted to me again in a conference in early 2003 when a pastor from a church in the Los Angeles area came to me and asked if I would pray for his leadership team. I agreed, so he brought over a group of eight people. I prayed for the first couple and the Holy Spirit gave me a prophetic word for the wife. I began prophesying, "I see you playing guitar, writing songs and..."

"That is not me, that is my husband," she interrupted. "He is our worship leader. I can't hold a tune in a bucket!"

"Lady, shut up!" I said, teasing her. "Do you know what prophecy is?"

"I guess I don't," she said, with a curious grin.

> *Grace can transform a mass murderer into a super-apostle.*

"Prophecy releases grace that creates gifts in your life that you have never had before," I said. "You will gain the ability to do things you couldn't do before the prophecy—if you believe. The Bible says that if you receive a prophet in the name of a prophet, you will receive a prophet's reward. But if you receive a prophet in the name of a righteous man you will only get a righteous man's reward. The value you place on the word determines the power you receive from it. It is important that you believe the word because Romans 12:6 says that the amount of grace you receive is determined by the proportion of *your* faith. Did you get that?"

> *The value you place on the word determines the power you receive from it.*
>
> ∿

"I think I did," she said with a smile.

"Good. Let's try it again." I began prophesying to her again. "I see you playing guitar, writing songs, and leading worship!"

"I receive that," she responded.

Nearly a year later, in another conference, the woman came up to me and asked, "Do you remember me?"

"No, I am afraid I don't," I said.

"You prophesied over me..." I must have had the question mark look on my face because she continued, "Oh, and you told me to shut up!"

We both laughed. "I remember that," I said.

"Well," she said with excitement in her voice. "I went home and learned to play the guitar in a couple of months. I have written several songs and now I lead worship in our 500-member church on Sundays!"

Talk about amazing grace—how sweet it made her sound. And she couldn't hold a tune in a bucket. The value you place on the word determines the power you receive from it.

SAVING GRACE

Not only can prophecy equip the saints with gifts and talents through the grace of God, it can also move pre-Christians from the eve of destruction to the doors of construction. When lost people are stuck in their sin, they don't need a prophetic proclamation that is a commentary on their failure. They already know they are screwed up. They need a violent act of grace that can blast them out of darkness and into life. The grace of God can also move pre-Christians from the eve of destruction to the doors of construction.

> *The grace of God can also move pre-Christians from the eve of destruction to the doors of construction.*

This became very clear to me on a plane ride home from Bakersfield, California. I was completely exhausted as my wife and I boarded the small plane. I told Kathy I would sit next to the window and try to catch a few minutes of sleep on the flight. As the plane left the ground I began to doze off, but the Lord interrupted my nap.

He asked, "Do you see that man at the end of the row?"

Opening one eye, I observed a large man across the aisle, three seats down from me. "Yes, Lord, I see him," I replied, fighting to stay asleep.

"I want to talk to him," He continued.

"Go ahead, Lord. You have my permission," I said, yawning.

"I want you to talk to him for Me!" He shot back with authority.

"Lord...no! Come on, Lord! I am so tired and I am the only prophet left!" I complained. I should have known better than to use that line on God, as it never did work for Elijah.

"Wake up, swap seats with Kathy, and do what I told you to do!" He said, pulling rank on me.

"Okay," I responded sheepishly.

I exchanged seats with Kathy and took a good look at the guy. He was a little over six feet tall. His head was completely shaved except for a ponytail that extended to his butt. His face was also shaved except for a goatee that went down to his bellybutton. He had tattoos all over his body, including large Chinese letters that went all the way around his head. He looked really mean!

"Okay, Lord, what do You want to say to this man?" I asked.

"Tell him he looks tough but he is a mama's boy," God responded.

"Lord! I am not going to tell him that!" I protested.

"Yes, you are!" the Lord said.

"What is the rest of the word?" I urged.

"Tell him that much and I will give you the rest," the Lord insisted.

So I leaned across the aisle and said, "I have a word from God for you." Now, I almost never tell people, "I have a word from God." I usually say something like, "I had a vision of you." But I was mad and tired.

He looked over at me and anxiety filled my heart. "What is it?" he asked.

"The Lord says you look tough but you're a mama's boy," I proclaimed.

"That's right," he said.

"You know why you're a mama's boy? Because your daddy left when you were a little boy," I told him, as confidence began to rise in my soul.

Stunned, he said, "You're right. My dad left and I have no relationship with him."

"What do you do for a living?" I asked.

"I am the bass guitar player for a heavy metal band called ————. Have you ever heard of it?"

"No, but you are not going to be in the band much longer because the band is going to break up before the end of the year. Do you know what you're going to do then?"

Prophecy is grace in action!

"I have no idea," he said. Prophecy is grace in action!

"You're going to travel the world starting orphanages and helping orphans. You were born to do this," I said. "You have an amazing heart for broken and lost children."

He was so moved that he raised his voice and said, "That is totally what I have wanted to do all my life."

The rest of this story would fill most of this book, but it was so amazing watching a punk rocker become a world missionary in one encounter with God. Prophecy is grace in action!

ANGELS ON ASSIGNMENT

The other way that forthtelling prophecy redefines our reality is through the ministry of the angels. The Psalmist wrote, *"Bless the Lord, you His angels, mighty in strength, who perform His word, obeying the voice of His word!"* (Ps. 103:20). The angels perform the word of God that is proclaimed by the voice of the Lord. God's angels become the agents of change whenever prophecies require events to be altered, things to be accomplished or wars to be won. The angels are the ones who are commissioned to carry out this type of prophecy. Hebrews says that the angels are servants to the children of God:

> *But to which of the angels has He ever said, "Sit at my right hand until I make Your enemies a footstool for Your*

feet?" Are they not all ministering spirits, sent out to ren-
der service for the sake of those who will inherit salvation?
(Hebrews 1:13-14)

When God needs to alter the circumstances to fulfill the word of the Lord, the angels are sent out to change them. Look at this story in Matthew's Gospel that drives this point home:

Now when they had gone, behold, **an angel of the Lord** *ap-*
peared to Joseph in a dream and said, "Get up! Take the
Child and His mother and flee to Egypt, and remain there
until I tell you; for Herod is going to search for the Child to
destroy Him." So Joseph got up and took the Child and His
mother while it was still night, and left for Egypt. He re-
mained there until the death of Herod. This was to fulfill
what had been spoken by the Lord through the prophet:
"Out of Egypt I called My Son" (Matthew 2:13-15).

I had firsthand experience with the angels in 1986 while we were living in Trinity County. A friend of mine, named Paul Schmidt, and I were ministering at our local convalescent hospital early every Sunday morning. Paul was a strong believer, a body builder, and a deputy sheriff. One morning we were standing outside the hospital praying before we went in to minister. As we prayed I heard myself say, "The Lord says that you are going to be the next sheriff of Trinity County!"

We were both stunned. Paul looked at me and said, "Wow, what was that about?"

"I am not sure," I replied.

In the months that followed, Paul decided to run for sheriff and I became his campaign manager. The county's law required him to quit the department to run for sheriff. We campaigned hard for months. The night of the primary election all the campaign workers went down to the courthouse to watch the Lord work through the election. We were hoping to cheer as we watched the election results come in by region. But there would be no cheering that night. When the night was over and all the results were in, Paul lost the primaries by a mile, coming in fourth out of nine candidates. We were brokenhearted. Our entire team left the courthouse crushed, crying and discouraged.

How could the Lord tell us that Paul was going to be the next sheriff of our county and then he didn't even get enough votes to be on the ballot? We were confused and devastated. I was personally feeling humiliated and guilty, thinking that I must have got the prophetic word wrong.

A few days later, very early on Saturday morning, our phone rang. Half asleep, I answered the phone and a voice on the other end said, "Hey, I am going to run for sheriff as a write-in candidate! What do you think?" It was Paul, and I was in no mood for more humiliation.

"I think you're *crazy*," I yelled into the phone. "You took fourth place when you were on the ballot. How would you have any kind of chance when people would have to remember to write you in? You're nuts!"

"God said I am supposed to be the next sheriff and I need to finish this race. Will you help me?" he pressed.

"I don't know," I replied. "I'll call you back later."

Paul did end up running as a write-in candidate and I continued being his manager. The week *before* the election we commissioned him as the next Sheriff of Trinity County at church.

On the day of the election, people were required to write his name on the ballot. We couldn't have any campaign signs anywhere within 1,000 feet of a polling place. To make matters worse, we had almost no money to run the campaign. There were no radio or TV ads. We just had some signs and a few newspapers ads. But when the race was over, Paul was the winner! The news reports read, "Paul Schmidt Wins Landslide Victory as a Write-In Candidate!"

Paul Schmidt Wins Landslide Victory!

Over the next several weeks, strange stories began to emerge from our community. Many people who went into the booths to vote for another candidate ended up having crazy experiences. Some said they couldn't get the lever on the machine to pull down and punch the card for either of the sheriff candidates so they decided to write Paul in. Others said that when they got into the booth, a voice spoke to them and said, "Write in Paul Schmidt!" Many had dreams the night before in which they were instructed to vote for Paul. Paul Schmidt Wins Landslide Victory!

Several citizens who came out with ads in the paper in support of one of the other candidates also had these experiences and changed their minds in the voting booth. These stories continued to emerge for months. Most of these people were not Christians. Paul became our sheriff and held the office for 16 years.

The question is, what really happened on that election day? Much like the days of Joseph and Mary, the Lord sent His angels to Trinity County to make sure the word that He prophesied to Paul Schmidt would come to pass. The angels were very busy that day. Some had to restrain the levers on voting machines. Others had to make sure people who insisted on voting for someone else couldn't leave their houses. There were angels who talked to people in the booths and angels who came to people in dreams. Heaven invaded earth that day and we all rejoiced in God's amazing ability to do miracles.

I learned a powerful lesson that year. You can alter the course of world history through prophetic declarations.

CHAPTER 11

Getting in the Flesh

∾

A NEW OPERATING SYSTEM

It was a warm summer night. I crawled into bed, exhausted from the day. Too many hours had passed since I had visited the restful solace of my own cot. My head fell to the pillow and continued to plummet deeper...deeper I tumbled, sleep engulfing my soul, into warm, living water flowing all around me, capturing me...slowing my descent...and I finally came to rest in the arms of God. There, in peaceful cohabitation with Him, far away from my busy life, an eternity removed from the cares of my temporary earthly dwelling, I rested, renewing myself in His radiant, warm embrace. Once more I had passed through the timeless veil, asleep to one world and awake to another, enjoying the fleeting moments of my vacation home a galaxy away...aware that someday I would slip into His eternity and never have to return. Once more I had passed through the timeless veil, asleep to one world and awake to another.

> *Once more
> I had passed
> through the time-
> less veil, asleep
> to one world
> and awake
> to another.*
>
> ❧

I love that world because there are no restrictions, no boxes, no straight lines, no limitations or impossibilities. Here earthly shadows find their living forms, reflections meet their substance, and truth is alive all around you. There are no dark veils or dimly lit rooms here; instead, light shimmering revelation is everywhere.

This is the realm where secrets are told, mysteries are revealed, and words have become worlds. Questions have answers and His perspectives transform your reality. Like entering a time machine and being thrust thousands of years into the future, you experience a realm that has no natural counterpart. When you awaken, you discover finite dictionaries bankrupt, incapable of articulating the limitless glory of His infinite creation. God's secrets are safe with you, for there are no words yet formed that capture the essence of His existence.

In this place I had a dream. I saw written *words* begin to flow in front of my eyes on something like a ticker tape running across a television screen. Words like *holy, true, powerful, peaceful,* and *godly* were moving from left to right across the screen. The words were flat and single dimensional, much like words typed on a piece of paper. I am releasing a new operating system!

Then suddenly a loud voice thundered from eternity, shouting, "I am releasing a new operating system! I am releasing a NEW OPERATING SYSTEM UPON MY CHURCH!"

This proclamation created its own picture, a kind of living PowerPoint. The scene changed and the *words* were now falling like rain all around me. But this time the *words* were multi-dimensional, like 3D but more, and alive. Some *words* were larger than other *words.* It was like you could see diverse aspects and perspectives of each *word* as you viewed it from different sides, sort of like looking at a car from the front, back, sides, and underneath. I stepped into the vision and began to breathe in the *words* as if they were oxygen. They were flowing in and out of me, forming the very attributes that each individual *word* contained. For example, when I breathed in the word ***peace***, I suddenly became a peaceful man. When I inhaled the word courage it assimilated into my being and become cellular in my soul. The word ***courage*** assimilated into my being and become cellular in my soul.

I am releasing a new operating system!

The *words* were alive with revelation. Everything I knew about each *word* now seemed elementary, hardly capturing the full essence of the meaning and impact of the real truth. The revelation and implications of the *words* were not so much in their definition as in their experience. Let me try to describe it like this. I could define the word *Corvette* to you intellectually, but if I gave you a ride at 180 miles an hour in my Corvette, the word *Corvette* would suddenly take on a whole new meaning. These definitions are not wrong, but they seem almost irrelevant in light of an experience. In this dream, every *word* became a vehicle traveling at the speed of light, illuminating celestial realities and casting shadows on my finite understanding.

The Lord spoke again and something like scales fell from my eyes as He leaned over and whispered in my ear, "I am about to unveil Myself before My people and expose them to depths of My glory that I have kept hidden, locked away in the vaults of Heaven from eternity past. Now I will emerge in splendor never before conceived, pass through the boundaries of human reason and be a crown of wisdom gracing the brows of My Beloved."

The Lord continued, "I am creating a new operating system that can contain My revelation, for the former wineskin will rip

> *The word courage assimilated into my being and become cellular in my soul.*
>
> ❧

under the weight of My Kingdom. The stagnant mind-sets of religious structures must give way to a living organism that can embrace My dreams and empower My people."

THE WORD IS ALIVE

Truth can be *introduced* by words but cannot be *reduced* to words. The writer of Hebrews makes it clear that the word is not ink on a page, but living and active:

For the word of God is living and active and sharper than any two-edged sword, and piercing as far as the division of soul and spirit, of both joints and marrow, and able to judge the thoughts and intentions of the heart (Hebrews 4:12).

Peter says we were born again by the living word of God:

You have been born again not of seed which is perishable but imperishable, that is, through the living and enduring word of God (1 Peter 1:23).

And Luke tells us that although Moses came down from the mountain with stone tablets, the words carved on stone were a sculpture of the living oracles. Much like a statue of a famous person chiseled out of rock, the stone tablets were not the substance of the living oracles but rather something like a commemorative plaque to them. Truth can be *introduced* by words but cannot be *reduced* to words.

This is the one who was in the congregation in the wilderness together with the angel who was speaking to him on Mount Sinai, and who was with our fathers; and he received living oracles to pass on to you (Acts 7:38).

The word of God was never meant just to be remembered, but also to be experienced and assimilated until it becomes flesh and walks among us as it did in the days of Jesus. If knowing the Bible were synonymous with knowing God, the Pharisees and Scribes would have rocked!

> *The Word became flesh, and dwelt among us, and we saw His glory, glory as of the only begotten from the Father, full of grace and truth* (John 1:14).

Having a relationship with God should never be mistaken for knowing the Scriptures. If knowing the Bible were synonymous with knowing God, the Pharisees and Scribes would have rocked! Jesus put it like this:

> *You search the Scriptures because you think that in them you have eternal life; it is these that testify about Me; and you are unwilling to come to Me so that you may have life* (John 5:39-40).

Bill Johnson says, "Some people believe that if you base your relationship with God on experience, you can fall into deception. But the truth is, if the Scriptures don't lead you into an experience with God, you are already deceived!" Randall Worley put it like this, "When we read the Scriptures without experiencing God, the Bible becomes the fourth member of the Trinity." You could burn every Bible on the planet and you still wouldn't be able to destroy the Word of God.

> *Truth can be introduced by words but cannot be reduced to words.*

You could burn every Bible on the planet and you still wouldn't be able to destroy the word of God. The word of God is not ink on a page. The word of God existed before ink was ever invented and long before man ever learned to read or write.

The Bible says, *"In the **beginning was the Word,** and the Word was with God, and the Word was God. He was in the beginning with God"* (John 1:1-2). Furthermore, Jesus made it clear that the word will be around long after earth has burned up and the heavens have evaporated. He said, *"Heaven and earth will pass away, but My words will not pass away"* (Luke 21:33). The Word of God is alive, organic, and indestructible. It can't be annulled, ignored, or altered. You can't break the word of God—it only breaks you. The Word of God is alive, organic, and indestructible. It can't be annulled, ignored, or altered.

When I first came on staff at Bethel Church, one of my responsibilities was to pick up our guest speakers at the airport. I didn't know most of the speakers, so my secretary would give me a picture and a little blurb about them. I needed to be able to recognize them and be acquainted with some of their history before they deplaned. So, for instance, if I were picking up Bobby Connors, I would put a picture of him in the front seat of my car. I didn't have Bobby Connors in the seat; I had a picture of him. The picture was there so that I would recognize Bobby when he got off the plane.

> *If knowing the Bible were synonymous with knowing God, the Pharisees and Scribes would have rocked!*

Many people know the Bible and think they know the Lord. The goal of the Scriptures is to lead us into a relationship with Jesus. A lot of people are driving around with a blurb and a picture of Jesus in the front seat of their vehicle of life, believing they're living a life of faith. It is sad because these people often get just enough of Jesus to be inoculated from the real thing! I received a fresh revelation of the living, active word of God from the dream and I felt convicted in my own soul that I had settled for an inferior relationship God.

ALL TRUTH IS NOT CREATED EQUAL

Remember in my dream I saw that some words were larger than other words and they carried more weight. I realized that part of God's new operating system is the revelation that all truth is not created equal, but there are actually levels of truth. For example, Paul writes, *"But now faith, hope, love, abide these three; but the **greatest** of these is love"* (1 Cor. 13:13). Did you notice that although faith is truth, hope is truth, and love is truth, God assigns the word "greatest" to love?

> *You could burn every Bible on the planet and you still wouldn't be able to destroy the Word of God.*

Jesus gives us another great example:

> *Woe to you, scribes and Pharisees, hypocrites! For you tithe mint and dill and cummin, and have neglected the weightier provisions of the law: justice and mercy and faithfulness; but these are the things you should have done without neglecting the others* (Matthew 23:23).

Jesus said that tithing is an important truth, which they should continue to do, but they neglected the *weightier* things of the law. Justice, mercy, and faithfulness are "heavier" truths than tithing! These "greater" and "weightier" truths create a kind of system of order. As I pondered my dream, I began to understand that truth out of order, context, and timing is perversion (the wrong version). Isaiah explained it like this. *"For precept must be upon precept, precept upon precept; line upon line, line upon line; here a little, and there a little"* (Isa. 28:10 KJV).

Let me give you an example. God created sex and He said it was "very good." But if you take sex out of its designed context, it suddenly becomes perversion, and it is no longer good but evil! What I am saying is that a "word" must be in its proper context to be true. The word *love* carries more weight than the word *justice*.

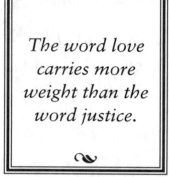

> *The word love carries more weight than the word justice.*

If you don't realize that the word *love* carries more weight than the word *justice*, you will be prone to destroy your relationships for the sake of creating justice. The result is that you will be "dead right," just like Noah's son, Ham, who was cursed for telling his brothers the truth about his father's sin.

HOW CULTS DEVELOP

God is beginning to release revelation of the levels of truth and their proper context so we don't create cults with new revelation. I now realize that many groups of Christians have embraced certain Scriptures with the wrong emphasis and have become cults living in perversion. The bigger problem, however, is that in most of these cases the Church has seen the perversion and reacted to the doctrine by virtually erasing it from their Bibles, resulting in an awesome revelation being lost forever, buried in the soil of heresy!

LIVING LEVELS

Applications for this revelation are exploding in me. I can see now that we have not understood the dimensions of truth, and therefore we have limited the application of the Scripture to its historic context and often even in this, created perversions that destroy people.

For instance, what happens when we lose sight of that fact that the word *love* is greater (carries more weight) than the word *submit?* We produce a family environment where wives are told to submit to their hateful, abusive husbands, often in the worst possible hell you can imagine. I am not advocating divorce here (that may be necessary in extreme cases); I am simply saying that Tarzan should have to live with the animals if he is going to act like one.

I have also watched many children flounder in the absence of discipline when their dads put friendship above fatherhood. Fatherhood becomes perverted because Dad is so concerned about being a friend to his kids that he is afraid to correct them. The result is that his sons and daughters enter adulthood completely unprepared to deal with authority figures in their lives. Their perverted perspective of authority will have to be adjusted in the harsh environment of the world instead of being molded by the firm but loving hands of their father.

FORMULA CHRISTIANITY

God gave me another dream in which I observed a man bottle-feeding a baby. Then I heard something like a court case going on in Heaven. The Judge emerged from His chambers and pronounced His decision: "No more formula Christianity!" He struck the bench with His gavel and lightning was released, destroying the baby's bottle.

The scene changed. Now the man was breastfeeding several children from his own breasts. The Judge made a second declaration, His decree echoing from the bench. "From now on My children will only be nourished from the milk that flows out of the life of the Body. From this day forward, My *word* must be experienced, assimilated, and digested by the Body, flow over the

> *"I never study to teach. I only study to learn."*
>
> ❧

heart, and out of the breast. Those who are breast-fed will always experience truth in the context of intimacy and transparency. No longer are My people to drink formula, simulated milk, man-made philosophies emerging from the mind, void of Spirit, ever learning doctrines not tested in the crucible of divine relationship, leading not to an experience with Me, absent of encounters, having a formula of godliness but denying My power!" "I never study to teach. I only study to learn."

Then I was carried away, back to my early years with Bill Johnson. He was reclining behind his desk with a serious expression on his face. His voice was stern, as if he was exhorting me over a life or death issue. *"I never study to teach. I only study to learn,"* he warned. (He used to say this to me all the time but I never really understood what he meant.) The view changed as if a camera had panned back for a wider shot. I immediately observed, among all the things on his desk, a 3x5 card standing upright with a message written on it. It read, *"Whatever feeds me feeds them."* I remember the saying so well but this time it was different. It seemed not to be coming from the card situated on Bill's desk but from the throne itself.

I awoke from the dream and my mind was vibrant with curiosity. Questions flooded my soul as if I had entered a room full of a thousand stimuli all simultaneously clamoring for my senses. I wondered at the ramifications of all this revelation. Scriptures emerged...inviting me to excavate past the soil of familiarity to promised secret treasures.

In the months that followed, the Bible became alive to me. Scriptures emerged from their pages, inviting me to excavate past the soil of familiarity to promised secret treasures. I became an archeologist, unearthing the mysteries of a long-lost Kingdom, searching for answers from a hidden civilization now veiled in traditions, doctrines, and theological hypotheses.

> *Scriptures emerged...inviting me to excavate past the soil of familiarity to promised secret treasures.*

BIBLICAL *KNOWING* INCLUDES EXPERIENCE

This dream led me to a series of observations. People who know the Scriptures and don't know God are the hardest folks to lead into a relationship with Christ. What they think they know keeps them from what they really do need to know. Biblical "knowing" is not the ability to recall facts but an *experience with* truth. A great example of the Bible's idea of "knowing" is the Book of Genesis. It says, *"Adam knew Eve his wife; and she conceived, and bare Cain"* (Gen. 4:1 KJV). The Hebrew word here is *yada*. It means that Adam experienced Eve. He didn't just know

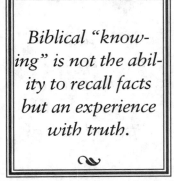

Biblical "knowing" is not the ability to recall facts but an experience with truth.

about her but he knew her intimately. Biblical "knowing" is not the ability to recall facts but an *experience with* truth.

Paul reiterated this principle when he wrote that God wants us to *"know the love of Christ which surpasses knowledge"* (Eph. 3:19). How can you know something that is beyond knowledge? Like *yada*, the Greek word "know" here means to "have an experience." Paul is telling us that to know God's love is to experience it in our heart, not define it with our minds.

Every *word* in the Bible is an invitation to experience a different reality. This is what I experienced in the first dream I shared, where breathing in each word created its own attribute in me. When I breathed in the *peace* I suddenly became a peaceful man, because this is the power of impartation that leads to transformation. Again, the revelation was not in the definition but in the experience. Every *word* in the Bible is an invitation to experience a different reality.

American culture has a core value that separates knowledge and experience. This is manifested in the educational system of our country, which primarily consists of filling the mind with information and getting people to remember facts. These schools often don't require their students to demonstrate that they can actually reproduce results. To make matters worse, it is not uncommon to have a professor who has never actually worked in the field of his expertise. For instance, it is typical to have a

> *Every word in the Bible is an invitation to experience a different reality.*

university business professor who has never worked in the business world. They learned the principles of business from a class, but have not been required to labor in the marketplace. These instructors reproduce *students*, not *disciples*. The folks that graduate from these institutions have knowledge but no experience.

Formula Christianity—represented by the bottle-feeding in the second dream—is fostered by this American mind-set. Leaders feed their people things they read in the Bible but they often haven't assimilated them into their own lives. They study to prepare a "sermon" but it is not a life message. This creates a cultural paradigm where "believing" means acknowledging or agreeing with a number of doctrinal statements. Because these sermons were not birthed in life experiences in the Kingdom they don't lead to relationship with the King. You can't reproduce in others what you don't posses yourself. You can teach what you know (not in the biblical sense of knowing), but you can only impart who you are. When leaders only teach what they know, it creates a cerebral culture where teachers and theologians wrangle over the meaning of the original text without experimenting with the ramifications of their reality to prove the manuscript. You can't reproduce in others what you don't posses yourself.

Jesus always connected believing with an experience. Look at the context of believing in the Book of Mark again:

> *He who has believed and has been baptized shall be saved; but he who has disbelieved shall be condemned. These signs will accompany those who have believed: in My name they will cast out demons, they will speak with new tongues; they will pick up serpents, and if they drink any deadly poison, it will not hurt them; they will lay hands on the sick, and they will recover* (Mark 16:16-18).

212

Jesus says if you believe, you will have an experience—there will be signs following you.

Paul makes it clear that the Kingdom *doesn't* consist of words but power. Words are the *invitation* to an experience but they are not the experience itself. Words are the *invitation* to an experience but they are not the experience itself.

> *You can't repro-duce in others what you don't posses yourself.*

Now some have become arrogant, as though I were not coming to you. But I will come to you soon, if the Lord wills, and I shall find out, not the words of those who are arrogant but their power. For the kingdom of God does not consist in words but in power (1 Corinthians 4:18-20).

When we replace Kingdom experiences with **words**, we wind up with religion. Paul warns Timothy about people who advocate this. He says they are *"holding to a form of godliness, although they have denied its power; avoid such men as these"* (2 Tim. 3:5).

When leaders do not create high expectation for an experience with God, they perpetuate a powerless culture. Even more troubling is that the people who live in this religious culture think they *have* experienced the Kingdom, so they stop "believing" for the real thing. Of course, when they stop having faith for an experience, they don't have one, which in turn validates that there is no experience beyond the assurance of their salvation. And the beat goes on and on, ultimately creating an experienceless lifestyle and culture.

> *Words are the invitation to an experience but they are not the experience itself.*

> *When we replace Kingdom experiences with words, we wind up with religion.*
>
> ❧

Articulation and demonstration were always meant to flow together in the Church. Nicodemus made this observation of Jesus: *"Rabbi, we know that You have come from God as a teacher; **for no one can do these signs that You do unless God is with him"*** (John 3:2). Nicodemus understood that Jesus was a teacher because His words had power.

THE GOAL OF TEACHING

Jesus said, *"A pupil is not above his teacher; but everyone, after he has been fully trained, will be like his teacher"* (Luke 6:40). The goal of true discipleship isn't that we would memorize the Bible but that we become like the One who teaches us—Jesus.

This is further emphasized in the parable of the sower. Jesus taught us that the Kingdom is planted in the lives of people like a sower plants seeds on his land. The three main characters (elements) in this play (parable) are the sower (God), the seed (the Kingdom), and the soil (our hearts). Let's look at one scene from this first century play.

> *The one on whom seed was sown on the rocky places, this is the man who hears the word and immediately receives it with joy; yet he has no firm root in himself, but is only temporary, and when affliction or persecution arises because of the word, immediately he falls away* (Matthew 13:20-21).

The Greek word for *seed* is the word *sperma*, which means "offspring." We get our English word *sperm* from this word. Notice how the sperm that falls on rocky soil is described as a man who has "no firm roots in himself." At first it seems odd that someone has to be prepared to receive the Kingdom, until you realize that the sperm of God cannot survive the hostile elements of this world.

I got a revelation of this a couple of years ago when Kathy and I went to Hawaii for the first time. As we began to drive our rental car down the highway in Maui, Kathy shouted, "Stop! Pull over!"

"What's wrong?" I asked.

"Do you see that huge tree on the side of the road? That is the plant we have in our bathroom!" (Our house looks like a jungle. Kathy **loves** plants.)

There is no such thing as an indoor plant.

"Great," I responded, trying to get my heart to stop bounding out of my chest.

We drove on a little farther. "Look over there," she said excitedly, pointing to another very large plant. "There is the plant we have on our kitchen sink."

"Wonderful," I conceded. This scene was repeated throughout our entire visit to the island.

It finally occurred to me that there is no such thing as an indoor plant. There are only plants created to live in another environment. When we take them out of their natural habitat, we have to create an artificial environment for them so that they will survive the elements. There is no such thing as an indoor plant.

In the same way, the sperm of God was created to live in another Kingdom. This world is a hostile environment to the life of God. His embryo needs a womb, an artificial environment that protects it from the elements, until the sperma of God grows into a man-child within us. By the way, we have been impregnated with Christ not through artificial insemination, but through immaculate conception. We have been impregnated with Christ through immaculate conception.

> We have been impregnated with Christ through immaculate conception.

Remember what Paul wrote to the Galatians? *"My children, with whom I am again in labor until Christ is formed in you"* (Gal. 4:19). How did Paul labor among them? Through teaching and preaching, of course. He was a sower, sowing the sperma of God into the wombs of His people. How is a womb formed so the seed of God can germinate and gestate within us? A womb is fashioned within us through instruction or in-struction.

"Wait a minute!" you say. "You just stated that you had to have a womb before you could receive God's teaching (sperma)! Now you are saying that instruction forms the womb. What's up with that?"

That's right, but teaching and instruction are two separate things. Let me explain. I described in the first chapter how the devil in trying to capture the epoch seasons through in-struction—fortresses built inside of people, which are constructed from thoughts, speculations, and lofty things (see 2 Cor. 10:4-5). These fortresses are built to protect satan's lies that grow like weeds inside of people, ultimately choking out the fruit of righteousness in society.

There are also castles built within us through in-struction that house the truths of God. Much like evil fortresses protect the lies of the enemy, these castles create a safe environment for the fetus conceived by God to be formed into Christ within us. There are also castles built within us through in-struction that house the truths of God.

The Hebrew and Greek words for *instruction* mean discipline, chastening, correction, punishment, reproof, and warning. The implication is that instruction is education or training through disciplinary action. It is no wonder that we are called disciples! The word *disciple* means "learner" but it comes from the word *discipline*. Solomon, describing a foolish person, said, *"How I have hated instruction! And my heart spurned reproof!"* (Prov. 5:12). Notice instruction is the fruit of reproof.

> *There are also castles built within us through in-struction that house the truths of God.*
>
> ❧

In the story of the sower, Jesus said the man had no roots in himself so the seed died. Roots are formed through the ability to receive instruction…structures within. If you refuse correction, reproof, discipline, and chastening, you won't have a womb to protect the seeds of teaching. Teaching comes from receiving information, or internal formation. We learned that it is Christ that is being formed with us, therefore teaching is the seed, and instruction forms the womb for it to grow in. Teaching comes from receiving information, or internal formation.

Over the years I have discipled lots of people. I have grieved many times over folks I have poured my life into who have later fallen away. For example, the person I spent the most time with in my whole life (besides my own family) no longer walks with God.

For years I used to meet with him at 6 A.M. before school to pray and encourage him. He became the leader of our campus ministry and led many kids to Christ. I led his wife to the Lord and was in his wedding. I was there when both of his children were born. I carried his seven-year-old daughter to the car with him the night Jesus touched her so deeply that she went into a trance. She shook all night under the power of God as the Lord showed her around Heaven.

This man has since divorced his wife, moved in with another woman and denounces God, saying he is an atheist.

> *Teaching comes from receiving information, or internal formation.*
>
> ∾

I have wept long hours over him. Looking back, I remember one thing about him that always troubled me. He never could take correction. He always had an excuse why things were not his fault. Now he has become a walking dead man who I will always love.

We must embrace the discipline of God that comes through human agency. It is life to our souls!

DEALING WITH THE DEVIL

Demonic powers have hijacked the Sword of the Spirit and used it to enslave the people of God for thousands of years. In doing so, they have unwittingly partnered with the very enemy they are trying to avoid.

Jesus, full of the Holy Spirit, returned from the Jordan and was led around by the Spirit in the wilderness for forty days, being tempted by the devil. And He ate nothing during those days, and when they had ended, He became hungry. And the devil said to Him, "If You are the Son of God, tell this stone to become bread." And Jesus answered him, "It is written, 'MAN SHALL NOT LIVE ON BREAD ALONE.'" And he led Him up and showed Him all the kingdoms of the world in a moment of time. And the devil said to Him, "I will give You all this domain and its glory; for it has been handed over to me, and I give it to whomever I wish. Therefore if You worship before me, it shall all be Yours." Jesus answered him, "It is written, 'YOU SHALL WORSHIP THE LORD YOUR GOD AND SERVE HIM ONLY.'" And he led Him to Jerusalem and had Him stand on the pinnacle of the temple, and said to Him, "If You are the Son of God, throw Yourself down from here; for it is written, 'HE WILL COMMAND HIS ANGELS CONCERNING YOU TO

GUARD YOU,' and, 'ON their HANDS THEY WILL BEAR YOU UP, SO THAT YOU WILL NOT STRIKE YOUR FOOT AGAINST A STONE.'" And Jesus answered and said to him, "It is said, 'YOU SHALL NOT PUT THE LORD YOUR GOD TO THE TEST.'" When the devil had finished every temptation, he left Him until an opportune time (Luke 4:1-13).

Here we see the devil using the Bible against Jesus in the wilderness. But the Bible is not always true! This is a shocking revelation, but it is very accurate. The word of God in the hands of the devil is actually the most destructive weapon known to man. The devil brought his greatest arsenal to this epic battlefield in the wilderness. Yes, that's right, he intended to destroy Jesus with His own Bible. He had probably been studying it for years to be ready to meet the Living Word in the desert. But the Bible is not always true! The Word of God in the hands of the devil is the most destructive weapon known.

> *But the Bible is not always true! The Word of God in the hands of the devil is the most destructive weapon known.*

The word of God in the hands of anyone besides the Holy Spirit always leads to religion, bondage, and death. Paul said, *"for the letter kills, but the Spirit gives life"* (2 Cor. 3:6).

WORD + SPIRIT = TRUTH

Automobiles were developed with a core assumption: *there will be fuel.* If the world ever ran out of fuel, a bicycle would be better transportation than a car. Owning something we could power ourselves would be better than transportation that required gas in a fuel-less world.

Contrary to popular belief, the Bible is not the best philosophy in the world because the Scriptures were written with the

> *The Holy Spirit is to the Scriptures what fuel is to the automobile.*
>
> ❧

core assumption that those who read it will have a relationship with the Holy Spirit. There are many philosophies that can be pedaled or powered by man and don't require God to make them work, but the Bible is not one of them.

Without the Spirit breathing on the word of God, much of the Scriptures don't work at all. They are just ink on a page, fuel-less philosophical vehicles. For instance, loving our enemies without a supernatural source of love and an understanding of divine justice is simply weakness to the world, and doing so is inviting exploitation. Dying so that we can live makes no sense at all unless there is supernatural life that replaces our old life. Laying hands on the sick so they recover is no more than a fairy tale without the Holy Spirit. The list goes on and on. The Holy Spirit is to the Scriptures what fuel is to the automobile. The word of God without the Spirit of God is not truth. The Spirit is the catalyst that takes the *word* and makes it into the truth. The Holy Spirit is to the Scriptures what fuel is to the automobile.

Jesus said:

> *But when He, the Spirit of truth, comes, He will guide you into all the truth; for He will not speak on His own initiative, but whatever He hears, He will speak; and He will disclose to you what is to come* (John 16:13).

Bill Johnson asks, "How can we have revival when we value a book the early Church didn't have over the Holy Spirit they did have?" I agree. I read my Bible every day and have for more than 30 years. I believe the Bible is the inerrant word of God. I believe every word of it is true. I believe that without a relationship with the Word of God we limit our potential in the Lord. But to develop a supernatural lifestyle we must let the Holy Spirit make the Word of God oxygen to our souls!

CHAPTER 12

Wisdom From Another World

It was a normal Sunday morning service. After the worship, prayer, and preaching, a team of us came to the front to minister to those who still needed a miracle. A lady in her mid-fifties waited patiently in line in front of me. Finally, after nearly an hour of waiting, she was next.

She described her illness to me—arthritis had filled her body and she was in pain everywhere. I laid my hands on her and began to command the arthritis to leave her body, but suddenly something strange happened.

The Holy Spirit said, "I am going to heal her through her husband. Have him come up and pray for her."

I stopped praying and asked, "Is your husband here?"

"Yes," she responded, very reluctantly.

"Have him come up here," I instructed.

Her body language clearly indicated that she was struggling with my request, but she finally went to the back of the sanctuary where he was seated. I could tell that they were having a heated exchange as she tried to convince him to join her for prayer. Her desperation apparently prevailed and he finally came to the front, his bad attitude in tow.

I tried to introduce myself to him but he wanted nothing to do with small talk so I got right to the point. "I want you to lay hands on your wife and God is going to use you to heal her," I proclaimed. (Actually, I was having a really hard time believing the Lord would use someone with such a bad attitude.)

The man turned white as a sheet and trembled with fear. "I can't do this!" he protested.

"Sure you can," I insisted. "I will tell you what to say and it will all work out just fine. I get paid big money to know this stuff," I joked, trying to lighten up the atmosphere. "Now put your hand right here," I demonstrated with my hand.

He followed me, still shaking like a leaf. "Now repeat after me, 'Arthritis, leave this body now!'"

He repeated my proclamation in a mousy tone that entirely lacked the confidence I had just demonstrated. I thought, *If this woman gets healed through this man it will rank among the greatest miracles I have ever witnessed.* But then something crazy happened. The lady began to weep and then wail. "What is it? What is going on?" I questioned anxiously.

> "He broke her, so he could fix her!" the Lord proclaimed.

"All my pain left! All my pain is gone! I am healed! I can't believe it—I am healed!" she shouted.

Her husband was stunned! He could hardly even speak. I tried to act confidently, like I knew all along she would get well, but I was as surprised as anyone.

When the service was finally over, I got in my car and began to make my way home, my mind flooded with questions. I couldn't wait any longer. I had to ask Him, "Lord, why did You heal that woman through her faithless husband instead of through me?"

His answer would forever change my ministry. "He broke her, so he could fix her!" the Lord proclaimed.

"He broke her, so he could fix her!" the Lord proclaimed. "If I healed her through you, her body would have gotten well, but if I healed her through him, I would begin the process of healing their marriage as well. She sees him as the harsh man she originally married," He continued. "Her bitterness towards him is killing her. Her husband has repented long ago but she can't see it. Now that she is healed through him, she will view him as part of the answer to her pain," He said.

TRIUNE RESTORATION

After this experience, I began to see that the Lord is not just interested in healing people's bodies. He is concerned with *how* their bodies get well. God showed me that it was His desire to heal the whole man. Consider this experience two of His disciples had with a lame man:

Now Peter and John were going up to the temple at the ninth hour, the hour of prayer. And a man who had been lame from his mother's womb was being carried along, whom they used to set down every day at the gate of the temple which is called Beautiful, in order to beg alms of those who were entering the temple. When he saw Peter and John about to go into the temple, he began asking to receive alms. But Peter, along with John, fixed his gaze on him and said, "Look at us!" And he began to give them his attention, expecting to receive something from them. But Peter said, "I do not possess silver and gold, but what I do have I give to you: In the name of Jesus Christ the Nazarene—walk!" And seizing him by the right hand, he raised him up; and

> When one member of our trinity is sick, it affects our entire being.
>
> ∽

immediately his feet and his ankles were strengthened. With a leap he stood upright and began to walk; and he entered the temple with them, **walking and leaping and praising** *God* (Acts 3:1-8).

The man walked because he got physically healed. He leaped because he got emotionally healed. And he praised God because he got spiritually restored! It's important for believers to realize that, like God, we are triune beings. We have a body, a soul, and a spirit. Furthermore, our trinity is so intertwined that it is impossible to separate each dimension of our being from the other. When one member of our trinity is sick, it affects our entire being. When we understand this, it makes sense that the Lord works to restore the whole man, because merely healing our bodies would only be a temporary, partial solution. If we and the people God has called us to minister to are going to come into true wholeness, it is essential that we understand how these triune life sources and systems interact with each other and how this affects our lives and the health of our being. What we need is divine wisdom. When one member of our trinity is sick, it affects our entire being.

THE TWO DIMENSIONS OF WISDOM

There are different kinds of wisdom in the world. There is the wisdom of *experience*, sometimes called the wisdom of the elders. This is the type of wisdom where people know what to do in various situations because they have been through it before. There is the wisdom of *education*. This is the ability to discern the best choice through training the intellect. But the wisdom of God is nothing like these. The wisdom of God is the ability to rightly apply knowledge in a way that builds for the future that which was envisioned by the Creator so that the divine ecosystem of Heaven yields life.

The wisdom of God has two dimensions. There is the wisdom from the mind of Christ and there is the wisdom that is a gift of the Holy Spirit. Let's look at each of these and see if we can move in some fresh insights ourselves.

THE SPIRITUAL GIFT OF WISDOM

The *gift* of wisdom, like the gift of healing, prophecy, or miracles, is a free endowment of the Holy Spirit. This kind of wisdom is not something we earn, but we get it by asking the Holy Spirit for it. It is the Spirit's gift to give away to whomever He wills. And like all the spiritual gifts, the Holy Spirit wills to give them to hungry and humble souls who ask for them.

Here is what Paul wrote about the gift of wisdom to the Corinthians:

> *But to each one is given the manifestation of the Spirit for the common good. For to one is given the word of wisdom through the Spirit, and to another the word of knowledge according to the same Spirit* (1 Corinthians 12:7-8).

Imagine you are in a hard situation, and you don't know what to do. Then it suddenly dawns on you—you have God living in you, the gift Master of the ages, the Divine Santa Claus of the universe, the most charitable Being to never have been created, the Captain of kind, the General of generous and the Boss of benevolent, and so on. You get the idea...He loves to give His kids gifts. So you decide to ask the Spirit for a word of wisdom for your situation and *wham*, all at once the Holy Spirit speaks to you and it changes everything. That's how the gift of wisdom works.

THE WISDOM FROM THE AGE TO COME

The spiritual gift of wisdom is not the only source of heavenly insight. We also have the wisdom from the age to come by possessing the mind of Christ, which we receive through rebirth. Look at the insights Paul had into Christ's wisdom:

For I determined to know nothing among you except Jesus Christ, and Him crucified. I was with you in weakness and in fear and in much trembling, and my message and my preaching were not in persuasive words of wisdom, but in demonstration of the Spirit and of power, so that your faith would not rest on the wisdom of men, but on the power of God. Yet we do speak wisdom among those who are mature; **a wisdom, however, not of this age** *nor of the rulers of this age, who are passing away; but we speak God's wisdom in a mystery, the hidden* **wisdom** *which God predestined before the ages to our glory;* **the wisdom** *which none of the rulers of this age has understood; for if they had understood it they would not have crucified the Lord of glory; but just as it is written,* "THINGS WHICH EYE HAS NOT SEEN AND EAR HAS NOT HEARD, AND *which* HAVE NOT ENTERED THE HEART OF MAN, ALL THAT GOD HAS PREPARED FOR THOSE WHO LOVE HIM." *For to us God revealed them through the Spirit; for the Spirit searches all things, even the depths of God. For who among men knows the* **thoughts** *of a man except the spirit of the man which is in him? Even so the* **thoughts** *of God no one knows except the Spirit of God. Now we have received, not the spirit of the world, but the Spirit who is from God, so that we may know the things freely given to us by God, which things we also speak, not in words taught by human wisdom, but in those taught by the Spirit, combining spiritual* **thoughts** *with spiritual* **words**. *But a natural man does not accept the things of the Spirit of God, for they are foolishness to him; and he cannot understand them, because they are spiritually appraised. But he who is spiritual appraises all things, yet he himself is appraised by no one.* **For WHO HAS KNOWN THE MIND OF THE LORD, THAT HE WILL INSTRUCT HIM? But we have the mind of Christ** (1 Corinthians 2:2-16).

Paul makes it clear in this passage that although the Old Testament people were ignorant of the things God wanted to do for them, the New Testament Saints have access to these mysteries because we have the mind of Christ. In other words, we think like God Himself!

What does this all mean to us practically? Every morning when we wake up, we view the world through the eyes of God. This mind-set is called the wisdom from the age to come. This timeless wisdom is necessary to capture the eternal purposes of the Alpha and Omega. Every morning we view the world through the eyes of God.

This *Holy Spirit's gift of wisdom* and the *wisdom of the age to come* need to work alongside the other spiritual gifts synergistically to maximize their restorative power. In this way we get insight into the whole man and the purposes of God. When we encounter someone who is sick, we need the dual dimensions of wisdom to be the one administering the *gifts of power*.

For example, someone might come to you to be healed of Lupus. Lupus is an autoimmune disease in which the white blood cells, which are supposed to attack the enemies of the body, instead destroy the body. I have learned that many times (not always) when people have problems in their soul (for instance, they don't like themselves), the brain gets the message that *they* are the enemy and uses their weapons against themselves, ultimately self-destructing. When you minister to these people using only the gift of healing, their bodies will typically get well for a short time, then relapse into sickness. In such cases the Lupus was a manifestation of something amiss in their soul, and although it affected the body, it was not rooted in their flesh.

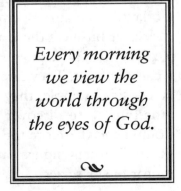

Every morning we view the world through the eyes of God.

Sometimes the opposite can happen, where the source of the sickness is

> *When we are equipped with the gift of wisdom, we understand the root causes and their prescribed cures by the Spirit.*

rooted in the body and it affects the soul and/or spirit. I experienced this firsthand a couple of years ago. I had a serious and painful colon problem (I will spare you the details) that lasted for months. I was in pain every minute of the day and night. As the months rolled on I began to get really depressed in my soul and spiritually very discouraged. But all this was rooted in the pain in my butt (pun intended). As soon as I got healed, **all** the other symptoms disappeared the same day.

The spirit world can also affect the body and the soul. When an evil spirit oppresses someone it often causes sickness and/or mental illness. It is important to know if the sickness has its source in an evil spirit or if the evil spirit is just being drawn to an infection in the soul like flies to dung.

When we are equipped with the gift of wisdom as well as the gift of healing, discernment, miracles, etc., we understand the root causes and their prescribed cures by the Spirit. This results in people getting whole and not just healed. When we are equipped with the gift of wisdom, we understand the root causes and their prescribed cures by the Spirit.

There is a great example of this in the automotive industry. I worked in the automotive repair business for many years. In the car repair business there are people who we negatively call "Parts Replacers." These guys are not technicians because they only fix what is broken. They rarely ask themselves *why* the particular part failed. For example, they replace a broken rocker arm on the engine but fail to discover that the lubrication system is malfunctioning and therefore the rocker arm is not being oiled. "Part Replacers" usually figure out that the engine isn't oiling when the motor finally seizes.

If we don't want to be the "Part Replacers" of the Kingdom then we have to learn how to flow in both wisdom and power.

MEDICINE

Christ-less medicine often ignores the triune aspects of our lives (spirit, soul, and body) as well as the multidimensional causes of illness, and thus is reduced to treating physical symptoms rather than addressing the deeper causes of these illnesses. Modern medicine is an extension of pop science, which often dilutes validity to that which is only detectable through natural observation. Some of these scientists render themselves ignorant of and irrelevant to the unfathomable discoveries of creation, having been washed up on the shores of human reason. Romans 1 says that creation is an expression of the Creator. But if you enter the discovery process with a presupposition (there is no God), you work to justify your reality instead of entering into a new one.

> *When psychiatrists limit their understanding to two-dimensional mind-sets, they frequently tranquilize symptoms instead of curing root causes.*

Let me make it clear that I don't believe that medicine and science are in themselves bad or wrong, nor do I think that all doctors and scientists are Christ-less. I am simply saying that *when* they are ignorant or resistant to the spirit realm they limit their process, discovery, and prescription to single dimensional mind-sets, which produce only symptomatic cures instead of true wholeness. When psychiatrists limit their understanding to two-dimensional mind-sets, they frequently tranquilize symptoms instead of curing root causes.

The same can be said of the field of psychiatry. When psychiatrists limit their understanding to two-dimensional mind-sets (the body and the soul) and refuse to acknowledge and embrace the spirit realm, they frequently tranquilize symptoms instead of curing root causes.

There is a deep call from the Lord to send Christians who walk in a supernatural lifestyle into these occupations so they can lead the way into new discoveries, innovations, and cures.

JESUS HEALED THE WHOLE MAN

Jesus always moved in the power of God, the wisdom of the Spirit and, of course, He had the mind of Christ (Duh!). This is why the Gospels are filled with Him performing multidimensional miracles. He wasn't just concerned with getting people healed but *how* they got healed. Although He healed thousands of people, details are only given for about 27 of His miracles, and what is amazing is that He used a different method for each miracle. Let's look at a few these miracles and see if we can glean some insights into how Jesus moved in wisdom and power to see the whole man restored.

Here is the popular story about the man at the pool of Bethesda:

> *Now there is in Jerusalem by the sheep gate a pool, which is called in Hebrew Bethesda, having five porticoes. In these lay a multitude of those who were sick, blind, lame, and withered, [waiting for the moving of the waters; for an angel of the Lord went down at certain seasons into the pool and stirred up the water; whoever then first, after the stirring up of the water, stepped in was made well from whatever disease with which he was afflicted.] A man was there who had been ill for thirty-eight years. When Jesus saw him lying there, and knew that he had already been a long time in that condition, He said to him, "Do you wish to get well?" The sick man answered Him, "Sir, I have no man to put me into the pool when the water is stirred up, but while I am coming, another steps down before me."*

Jesus said to him, "Get up, pick up your pallet and walk." Immediately the man became well, and picked up his pallet and began to walk. Now it was the Sabbath on that day. So the Jews were saying to the man who was cured, "It is the Sabbath, and it is not permissible for you to carry your pallet" (John 5:2-10).

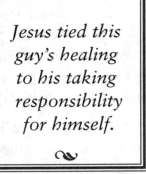

Jesus tied this guy's healing to his taking responsibility for himself.

Notice that Jesus asked the man a direct question: "Do you want to get well?" Instead of answering the question, the man gave the Lord several excuses (none of which were his fault) for why he wasn't already well. If you were sick for 38 years, wouldn't you want to get well?

Maybe you would but maybe you wouldn't! Let's look a little a deeper into this story. First of all it is important to note that the man is not named. His name is not important in the story because his real identity is in his crisis, not in his Christ. He has developed a victim's mentality ("No one cares about me...wa, wa, wa."). Secondly, remember that this man had never worked in his entire life. Getting healed meant he had to become responsible to provide for himself. He would no longer be the recipient of others' sympathy. He had no job skills and had never been accountable for anything.

So pay close attention to *how* Jesus healed him. "Take up your pallet and walk!" He commands. It seems a little rough to tell a person who has never walked in his entire life to get up and clean up his mess. But Jesus tied this guy's healing to his taking responsibility for himself. Therefore his physical healing is a direct result of his ability to work. Of course, the religious spirit doesn't allow this man to work for his healing, saying, "It is not permissible for you to work on the Sabbath." Jesus tied this guy's healing to his taking responsibility for himself.

There are lots of reasons why people don't always want to be healed. I remember walking into Denny's Restaurant at midnight a few years back. We had just finished doing a conference on the coast of California, and we had decided to get something to eat. A rough-looking dude yelled for me to come to his table. I walked over there and realized he was steaming mad.

"You're the preacher who spoke in that conference tonight, aren't you?" he snapped.

"Yeah!"

"Well, I got a real problem with you, buddy!" he said.

"What's the problem?" I asked cautiously.

"My friend talked me into coming to your meeting and one of your team prayed for my knees," he said, nearly yelling.

"So what is the problem?" I asked again.

"I got healed tonight," he responded. "Tomorrow I go to court for the final time for an accident I was in several years ago. My knees were destroyed in the accident and I am suing for a million dollars. But now that my knees are healed, I am going to have a hard time proving I was really injured. Now, what am I going to do?"

"Well, I got an idea," I said, looking right into his eyes. "We can ask God to take your healing back and then you will win your case."

He looked stunned. He thought for a minute and said, "No. They couldn't pay me a million dollars to live in that pain again."

LEPERS RESTORED

Here are two more amazing miracles where wisdom and power flowed together to restore people's lives:

While He was in one of the cities, behold, there was a man covered with leprosy; and when he saw Jesus, he fell on his face and implored Him, saying, "Lord, if You are willing, You can make me clean." And He stretched out His hand and touched him, saying, "I am willing; be cleansed." And immediately the leprosy left him. And He ordered him to tell no one, "But go and show yourself to the priest and make an offering for your cleansing, just as Moses commanded, as a testimony to them" (Luke 5:12-14).

As He entered a village, ten leprous men who stood at a distance met Him; and they raised their voices, saying, "Jesus, Master, have mercy on us!" When He saw them, He said to them, "Go and show yourselves to the priests." And as they were going, they were cleansed (Luke 17:12-14).

Why did Jesus reconnect the lepers with the priest as a part of their healing? The answer is simple. If you had leprosy, you were not only physically ill but you were also spiritually rejected. The priests were the ones charged with reinforcing the harsh law against the unclean. They proclaimed judgments in the name of Jehovah that made sick people physical, emotional, and spiritual outcasts. I would imagine that most lepers hated the priest. But Jesus used the priest as part of the restoration process so that lepers would see them as a necessary part of their lives, thus restoring their physical and spiritual beings simultaneously. Jesus restored their souls by touching them.

When Jesus ministered one-on-one with lepers He would also touch them. They had never had anyone lay a hand on them before because they were contagious. Jesus restored their souls by

Jesus restored their souls by touching them.

touching them, their bodies by healing their leprosy, and their spirits by reconnecting them with the priest.

SPIT IN YOUR EYE

Here is an interesting and slightly disgusting example of a multidimensional miracle:

> *As He passed by, He saw a man blind from birth. And His disciples asked Him, "Rabbi, who sinned, this man or his parents, that he would be born blind?" Jesus answered, "It was neither that this man sinned, nor his parents; but it was so that the works of God might be displayed in him. We must work the works of Him who sent Me as long as it is day; night is coming when no one can work. While I am in the world, I am the Light of the world." When He had said this, He spat on the ground, and made clay of the spittle, and applied the clay to his eyes, and said to him, "Go, wash in the pool of Siloam" (which is translated, Sent). So he went away and washed, and came back seeing* (John 9:1-7).

When someone in America has a disability, most people feel sorry for them. But it was different among the Jewish people of Jesus' day. The Jewish people believed that when someone had a debilitating illness, God had cursed them. This explains the disciples' question, "Who sinned, this man or his parents?" It would be common for Jewish people to show contempt for sick people as a way of agreeing with God. Spitting on someone was the ultimate public humiliation. This blind man had probably been spit on many times before. When he heard Jesus spit on the ground I am sure he was bracing himself for the worst, but this was last time he would ever hear someone spit on his behalf. This time the noise associated with humiliation was used to enact his

> *This time the noise associated with humiliation was used to enact his healing!*
> ∾

healing! This time the noise associated with humiliation was used to enact his healing!

LIVING FROM THE THIRD HEAVEN

The wisdom of God thinks from eternity and realizes that we are a part of a divine economy in which the actions in one realm have a direct counteraction in another. The human race coexists among other created spiritual beings that have an agenda for us and live on the sight side of one-way glass. Those without the mind of Christ look into the glass and tend to only see their reflection, often drawing the wrong conclusion that we inhabit other than cohabit this planet. But the truth is we are not alone!

Not only are we triune beings but we are also alive in a three-dimensional realm, or heaven. There is the first heaven, which came into being when God created the heaven and the earth. There is the second heaven that the devil and his demons control. This is clearly articulated in the Book of Ephesians. It reads:

> *For our struggle is not against flesh and blood, but against the rulers, against the powers, against the world forces of this darkness, against the spiritual forces of wickedness **in the heavenly places*** (Ephesians 6:12).

And finally, there is the third heaven where God lives and rules from. Paul visited this place and wrote to the Corinthians about it. Here is his account of the visit:

> *I know a man in Christ who fourteen years ago—whether in the body I do not know, or out of the body I do not know, God knows—such a man was caught up to the **third** heaven. And I know how such a man—whether in the body or apart from the body I do not know, God knows—was caught up into Paradise and heard inexpressible words, which a man is not permitted to speak* (2 Corinthians 12:2-4).

The visional empire lives at the mercy of the greater realms of Heaven. To be blind to the spirit realm, that is, to be ignorant of two of the three realms of heaven, creates a kind of reactionary existence that relegates the human race to puppets hanging from the strings of spiritual manipulation. It is imperative that we understand the metron, core effect, and mission that the second heaven has over the world so that we can annul its effect on the human race while we extend the borders of the Kingdom. The visional empire lives at the mercy of the greater realms of Heaven.

Many perceive life like a checker game in which we are playing the game of life on a single-dimensional checkerboard. But the truth is that *we are the pieces* being played in a kind of three-dimensional chess game. Not only do we have to concern ourselves with the other players on the lower board; but the chess pieces on the second and third levels have power over the first level chessmen.

When we tap into the mind of Christ we are elevated to the third heaven and live with perspective and power that transcend the lower boards (heavens). Suddenly we are living with the wisdom from the timeless zone and are no longer victims of demonic schemes. Instead we become partakers of the priestly process. We become partakers of the priestly process.

> *The visional empire lives at the mercy of the greater realms of Heaven.*
>
> ❧

Not only does this process transform us, but God's wisdom causes us to outwit and destroy the demonic plots and plans that are devised against us. Living with the wisdom from the age to come reminds me of the old cartoon series of the Roadrunner and the Wile E. Coyote. The Coyote would set a trap to destroy the Roadrunner but the Roadrunner always outsmarted him (beep beep). The cartoon always ends with Wile E. caught in his own trap or blowing himself up with the dynamite he intended for the bird. The Roadrunner was giving that coyote a lesson in wisdom.

Paul talked about the Church teaching the wisdom of God to the rulers and authorities in heavenly places. It seems awesome to me that God has given us His authority to overpower the second heaven and His wisdom to outsmart them. Here it is in Paul's own words.

> *To me, the very least of all saints, this grace was given, to preach to the Gentiles the unfathomable riches of Christ, and to bring to light what is the administration of the mystery which for ages has been hidden in God who created all things; so that the* **manifold wisdom of God might now be made known through the church to the rulers and the authorities in the heavenly places** *(Ephesians 3:8-10).*

We become partakers of the priestly process.

Jesus demonstrated this wisdom in dealing with the coyotes of hell. He always seemed to avoid their traps while they would get entangled in their own devices. One of the most vivid pictures of the wisdom of God working through the life of Jesus is buried in the story of the woman caught in adultery. We already discussed the Pharisees' judgmental attitude earlier in the book. Now let's take a fresh look at this old story:

> *The scribes and the Pharisees brought a woman caught in adultery, and having set her in the center of the court, they said to Him, "Teacher, this woman has been caught in adultery, in the very act. Now in the Law Moses commanded us to stone such women; what then do You say?" They were saying this, testing Him, so that they might have grounds for accusing Him. But Jesus stooped down and with His finger wrote on the ground. But when they persisted in asking Him, He straightened up, and said to them, "He who is without sin among you, let him be the first to throw a stone at her." Again He stooped down and*

wrote on the ground. When they heard it, they began to go out one by one, beginning with the older ones, and He was left alone, and the woman, where she was, in the center of the court. Straightening up, Jesus said to her, "Woman, where are they? Did no one condemn you?" She said, "No one, Lord." And Jesus said, "I do not condemn you, either. Go. From now on sin no more" (John 8:3-11).

Jesus had a major challenge on His hands here because if He showed the woman mercy and let her go, He would break the law He came to fulfill. If He condemned her, then He would undermine His own message: *"For God did not send the Son into the world to judge the world, but that the world might be saved through Him"* (John 3:17).

When the religious leaders pressed Him for an answer, He stunned them with His wisdom. "Let him who has no sin get the stoning started," He proclaimed. Then He wrote in the sand. (I have always believed that He wrote each one of the religious leaders' names in the sand with a list of their latest sins next to them.)

Conviction entered their hearts and not one of them could bring himself to start the stoning. In one question Jesus transformed the Pharisees and scribes from judgmental jerks to convicted sinners. Now the very people who wanted the adulteress punished wished for her release as they pondered their own plight with sin. I have a feeling that these religious leaders stayed near enough to perceive Jesus' attitude towards her debt, because they needed a savior themselves (beep...beep).

RULING WITH WISDOM

I opened this book with an epic cry for the Bride of Christ to arise to her high call in God and begin to disciple the nations of the world. In my exhortation to you I quoted Daniel chapter 7, which says:

Then the sovereignty, the dominion and the greatness of all the kingdoms under the whole heaven will be given to the people of the saints of the Highest One; His kingdom will be an everlasting kingdom, and all the dominions will serve and obey Him (Daniel 7:27).

Nine months later, while writing this final chapter I became overwhelmed by Daniel's prophecy from long ago. The statement that the saints were to govern "all the kingdoms under the whole heaven" especially intrigued me. What struck me was that he didn't say, *all the kingdoms on the earth.* This prophecy is obviously a kind of *back to the future* proclamation, an intentional reconnection to our original mandate in the garden. It was there that God created us with our cosmic purpose and completed the circle of life. Here are the Creator's words that became flesh in us. It was there that God created us with our cosmic purpose and completed the circle of life.

Then God said, "Let Us make man in Our image, according to Our likeness; and let them rule over the fish of the sea and over the birds of the sky and over the cattle and over all the earth, and over every creeping thing that creeps on the earth" (Genesis 1:26).

Man's original mission in life was to rule the fish, the birds, the animals, and every creeping thing that creeps on the earth. The commission to disciple nations and rule over all the power of the enemy was added to our mandate after creation. Here is a list of some of the kingdoms under the whole heaven that we are called to govern:

> *It was there that God created us with our cosmic purpose and completed the circle of life.*

✧ The kingdoms of men

✧ The kingdom of darkness

✧ The bird kingdom

- ✧ The marine kingdom
- ✧ The animal kingdom
- ✧ The insect kingdom
- ✧ The biological kingdom

I am not sure how we are supposed to "rule" birds, fish, or insects much less the biological kingdom, but I have a sense that the wisdom we have been talking about in this chapter is going to lead us into new revelation of our divine destiny.

Jesus made an interesting statement that has always fascinated me. He said, "Go into all the world and preach the gospel to *all creation.*" I have always wondered why we were told to preach the gospel to **all creation** and not just to people. To make matters even more interesting, the apostle Paul had this insight into creation.

> *For the anxious longing of the creation waits eagerly for the revealing of the sons of God. For the creation was subjected to futility, not willingly, but because of Him who subjected it, in hope that the creation itself also will be set free from its slavery to corruption into the freedom of the glory of the children of God* (Romans 8:19-21).

I began asking for insight into creation's dilemma. I thought of the corruption I have seen take place among mankind. I remembered this last year when storms destroyed much of New Orleans and the police were unable to get into the neighborhoods for several days. What took place in the absence of authority was stunning. Looters broke into houses and stores, stealing everything they could get their hands on. Chaos and crime filled the streets as people ran wild, transforming the city into a war zone, a living hell.

The prophet Isaiah said, *"There will be no end to the increase of His government or of peace..."* (Isa. 9:7). Peace is the ultimate outcome of the government of God leading the kingdoms of this world. As we saw in New Orleans, when government is absent, injustice reigns supreme.

I wonder if creation's corruption is like the police-less streets of New Orleans. Is it possible, for instance, that most sickness is a manifestation of the biological kingdom in disarray because the ones (saints) who have been called to govern the biological kingdom have been AWOL or maybe we just have not had the wisdom to lead "all the kingdoms under the whole heaven" yet? After all, it is the blood of Jesus that saved us and set us free from all sin. Blood is a part of the biological kingdom. In other words, our redemption was initiated in the biological realm and then is supposed to spread to the rest of the creation.

I have a sense that God's emphasis in this next season is going to transition from healing (getting people well) to divine health as we begin to apprehend the mysteries of the kingdom.

We need the wisdom of the age to come to give us insight into creation's predicament. It is only in the age to come that there is no sickness, sadness, or crime. We have been commanded to pray that it would be on earth as it is in heaven (the age to come). It is incumbent upon us as the people of God to walk in the power of God, receive the wisdom of God, and do the works of God until the Kingdom of God comes here on earth as it is in Heaven—the third heaven that is! This is the greatest story ever told and it is the mandate of all those who want to develop a supernatural lifestyle.

Epilogue

Each and every day the world wakes up to the bad news of a planet in decay. Everywhere depression and death seem to be pressing into our minds and stealing away our courage. Even our homes that were once safe places for children to grow up in love have become, for many, battlefields where little ones must run for cover.

Yet in all of this confusion there is still a God who only rested one day. He was the one who spoke this world into being and declared it to be "very good"—a declaration that perpetuates to this day. It is He who reigns supreme over all of His creation. He is not depressed, confused, afraid, or perplexed over the darkness of this planet. He still speaks into those who are formless and void and creates life with His words!

I know a man who, 25 years ago, had a nervous breakdown. The breakdown lasted for more than three-and-a-half years. His hands trembled so violently that he could not even bring a glass of water to his lips without using both hands. He would sweat so profusely at night from fear and anxiety that his wife would have to get up in the middle of the night and change the soaking wet sheets. As time went on he began to lose his mind and many times a day he would envision himself murdering people—or worse. Demons started visiting him and tormenting him throughout the night.

Then, one afternoon, some men persuaded him to attend a Christian retreat in the mountains. That day a prophet was speaking at the meeting. He called the young man out of the crowd and prophesied to him. He said, "The Lord has called you to be a pillar in the house of God. You shall be a teacher and a leader of His people. Strength is in you!"

The war in that man's life was won that day through a creative declaration. I know that man very well, for I am that man!

Never underestimate the redemptive power of God's supernatural ministry. So many people are starving to know who they really are. You have the ability to alter the history of people who are lost in darkness and broken beyond repair. Hell's trash is becoming Heaven's treasures.

Don't Disappoint Them!

In the Beginning—Developing a Supernatural Lifestyle

Some of our new friends who are reading this book may have no idea how to get started in your life with Jesus. I thought I would take a moment to explain where to begin.

The Bible makes it clear that all of us are in need of a savior…someone to pay for our sins so that we don't have to live a life of bondage and torment. Jesus died on the cross for us and He also died *as us*. He took on the penalty for all the stuff we have ever done wrong and ever will do wrong. Jesus wants to do more than forgive us though; He wants to give us a brand-new life in the Kingdom of God right now on this earth and He desires to take us to Heaven when we pass on from this life to the next. If that isn't good enough, there is more… He has promised that when we ask Him into our hearts that we will be "Born Again" and become a new creation. He gives us a new life with a new heart and a new mind. You read about much of this in the book.

What do you have to do to begin this amazing life with God? Good question. You need to ask Jesus to come into your life and be your leader and your savior. You need to be willing to give the leadership role of your life to Jesus and be serious about following Him.

You need to acknowledge that you have sinned and need His help to change. And you need to ask Him to forgive you and you need to forgive everyone who has hurt you.

If you are willing to do these things to follow Jesus, I want you to pray this prayer with me:

> Jesus, I have done a lot of things wrong in my life that I need You to forgive. I am sorry for the life that I have led without You in my heart. From now on I want to follow You and let You be in charge of my entire life. I am ready to forsake my old life and take on Your life, Your ways, and Your desires. I will forgive anyone who has harmed or hurt me and allow them to live free from my revenge. I ask You to send Your Holy Spirit into my life and baptize me with His love and power. Amen!

Now find a good church that you can grow in and go there as often as you can. Look for someone who is mature in God to mentor you...sometimes this happens naturally in home groups. Read your Bible daily (start in the Book of John)...ask the Holy Spirit to teach you as you read. Take time to pray every day, listening for Jesus to speak to you as you seek Him, and last of all, share your life with others.

May the King of Glory meet you in the palace of your dreams as you begin this new life in the Kingdom of God!

Love,

Kris Vallotton

Bethel School of Supernatural Ministry

Bethel School of Supernatural Ministry is dedicated to worldwide transformation through spiritual revival. We are training and equipping the Body of Christ to bring the love of God and power of the Holy Spirit into the darkest places of the planet and establish Holy Spirit fortifications, resulting in the kingdom of this world becoming the Kingdom of our God.

BSSM is more than a school; it's a Holy Spirit journey into the realm of the impossible, a heavenly adventure where no one dare travel without God. In this haven of love, you will learn how to minister with power, and walk in signs and wonders.

Kris Vallotton—Senior Overseer and Founder

Other books and tapes
by Kris Vallotton

- ✧ The Supernatural Ways of Royalty
- ✧ Basic Training for the Prophetic Ministry
- ✧ Attributes of Royalty
- ✧ Developing a Legacy
- ✧ Fighting for Your Place in History
- ✧ For the Love of God
- ✧ From Paupers to Princes
- ✧ Purity
- ✧ Seven Pillars of Society

These and many other titles are available at:
www.kvministries.com, www.ibethel.org,
or call 530-246-6000.

Books and tapes by Bill Johnson

✦ Strengthen Yourself in the Lord

✦ When Heaven Invades Earth

✦ The Supernatural Power of a Transformed Mind

✦ How to Overcome Disappointment

✦ Mission Possible

✦ Revolution: Erasing the Lines between the Secular and the Sacred

✦ Healing: Our Neglected Birthright

✦ The Advancing Kingdom: A Practical Guide to the

✦ Normal Christian Life of Victory and Purpose

✦ Leading from the Heart

✦ The Quest: For the Face of God

✧ From Glory to Glory: Biblical Patterns for Sustaining Revival

These and many other titles are available at:
www.BillJohnsonMinistries.com, www.ibethel.org,
or call 530-246-6000.